WORKING WITH
THE DYING AND GRIEVING

VALERIE YOUNG

INTERNATIONAL DIALOGUE PRESS • DAVIS • CALIFORNIA

Library of Congress Card Number - 84-81131
ISBN 0-89881-018-3

THIS BOOK IS DEDICATED TO
THE KARA COUNSELORS

AUTHOR

VALERIE YOUNG, Ph.D., is the director of the counseling program at Kara in Palo Alto, California, where she trains and supervises counselors who work with individuals who have life threatening illnesses or are grieving. She has also led groups and conducted workshops on working with the dying and grieving for graduate students in psychology, social workers, therapists, nurses, and other caregivers of the terminally ill.

PREFACE

I was inspired to write this book when I began my work, almost six years ago, as Director of the counseling program at Kara, a nonprofit organization providing counseling for the terminally ill and grieving. I could not at the time find a satisfactory source of comprehensive information and exercises for training counselors.

I believe that in order to work with the dying and grieving, a person needs to learn to pay close attention and to listen carefully. He should be willing to look at pain with open eyes and have some understanding of his own relationship with death and grief. This book brings together what I have learned from the staff, consultants, and counselors at Kara and from a wide variety of sources in the field. It also reflects my personal commitment to respond to and support that which is essential in both myself and others.

Developing the quality of presence and the attention skills needed to work with the dying and grieving can help each of us to live life as fully and consciously as possible. Death often causes counselors, clients, and family members to face and test the rules that they have followed in life and to examine them in the face of the ultimate indifference of the universe. Death can cause a person to buckle under with feelings of impotence or helplessness, or it can serve to help him find the core of his being and learn how it is connected with the universe. One goal of this book is to teach the counselor to explore these emotions personally and to learn how to support others in their own process of coming to terms with life and death.

One of the most important aspects of the training for counselors (and for trainers) is the potential for a personal exploration of how one has chosen to live one's life. The counselor may learn to understand his smaller losses differently. He may discover the difficulty and joy of surrendering, and learn that what matters is the essential connection with himself and others. The encounter with death often dissolves pretense and challenges a person's assumptions about life. Learning to counsel the dying and grieving can further a person's exploration of who he truly is, what his purpose is, and what values he may choose to live by. Attitude shifts such as these will, in turn, enrich his relationships with dying and grieving clients.

I work with the dying and grieving every day and have become aware that I spend most of my waking moments knowing in the back of my mind that I will die. Why does anyone choose to do this work? Death and pain are constantly in the foreground, yet those who choose to counsel the dying often find that it is a way to experience faith, love, and truth. In looking at this volume, I feel that the underlying theme is love. Training people to listen and respond to those who are dying or grieving involves teaching them to experience love in its most essential form. The practice of counseling the dying and grieving is one of saying "yes" unconditionally to everything that arises for the client, and "yes" just as many times to oneself. Such affirmation means loving ourselves and others for being simply who we are, accepting our mistakes and celebrating our successes. Working with the dying and grieving means saying "yes" to all our attempts to make sense of life, to the fear in each of us, and to our attempts to hide, ignore, run from, or transcend it. Finally, it means saying an awe-filled "yes" to the universe that unfolds its miracles every day. Even if these miracles are ignored, avoided, or misunderstood, it continues to dust us with them anyway.

Valerie Young
Menlo Park, Ca.
March, 1984

CONTENTS

FIGURES

TABLE

EXERCISES

ACKNOWLEDGMENTS

I want to thank Carol Lillibridge, the Executive Director of Kara, the other staff at Kara, and the Kara counselors for their support and flexibility as I wrote this book. This very special group of people created the foundation of Kara, its unique philosophy, its humanistic administrative structure, and its counselor guidelines and procedures that help us to do this work so effectively. I also want to thank the many unidentified Kara clients who express themselves so poignantly throughout the book. Deep appreciation goes to Connie Cavanaugh, James Fadiman, Ph.D., Arthur Hastings, Ph.D., Kathleen Speeth, Ph.D., Susan Light, Robert Lincoln, Ph.D., and John Black, Ph.D., for their inspiration, assistance, and feedback. I am indebted to Betty Dickman, Marie and Don Anthony for their long hours of typing, and to Nora Harlow for her editorial assistance in transforming the original dissertation into a book. And lastly, I thank Ernst Wenk for standing by me and seeing this project through to publication.

My appreciation is more deeply felt than these words express. I now understand why most books have this separate page for acknowledgments. I am grateful for the support I have received from my community and realize more fully that no creation can be formed from a purely solitary state.

NOTE

All names and identifying features of Kara clients quoted or described in this volume have been altered to protect their anonymity. Any close resemblance to persons living or dead is not intended.

The masculine pronoun has been used throughout for the sake of simplicity and ease of reading. Two-thirds of both clients and counselors at Kara are women, and there is no intention to ignore this fact or to deny the feminine side of our nature.

PERMISSIONS

I would like to thank the following for permission to reprint material in this book:

"Confronting the Existential Meaning of My Death through Exercises," *Interpersonal Development*, 1973, *4*, pp. 148-163. Copyright © by James Bugental, Ph.D. Reprinted by permission.

PART I

RESEARCH AND THEORY

CHAPTER ONE

INTRODUCTION

This book is part of a two-volume work intended as a resource for volunteer and professional caregivers who work with the dying and grieving. The companion volume, entitled *Working with the Dying and Grieving: A Trainer's Manual,* is oriented to those who train counselors and caregivers to work with dying or grieving patients or clients. The present volume is designed for the trainee, or as a stand-alone guide for lay people who want to learn more about this important subject. Both books draw heavily from the author's experience as Director of Counseling at Kara, a nonprofit, largely volunteer organization that provides emotional support without charge to people who are living with life-threatening illness such as cancer or grief from suicide, terminal illness, accidental death, or homicide.

Because this book resulted from the author's psychologically oriented work at Kara, the words "counselor" and "client" are used throughout. Yet the book is written for anyone who works with or cares for people who are dying or grieving. The book presents the basic material needed to enable a person to provide adequate emotional support to the terminally ill or grieving, but it is expected that those who provide such support may also be offering medical, psychological, or spiritual services as well. Readers thus will include physicians, nurses, clergy, therapists, peer counselors, hospice workers, and family and friends of those who are dying or grieving.

KARA

The name Kara comes from the Gothic *kara,* which means lament. Henri Nouwen describes the caring person as one who shares our pain without feeling that he or she must do something about it, and this definition of care underlies the support offered by Kara counselors:

> When we honestly ask ourselves which persons in our lives mean the most to us, we often find that it is those who, instead of giving much advice, solutions, or cures, have chosen rather to share our pain and touch our wounds with a gentle and tender hand. The friend who can be silent with us in an hour of grief and bereavement, who can tolerate not-knowing, not-curing, not-healing, and face with us the reality of our powerlessness, that is the friend who cares.[1]

Kara's purpose is to support individuals and families in a caring and nonjudgmental manner. The organization trains volunteers to work with the dying and grieving, providing these services without charge to the client. Kara also offers support groups to professionals who work with dying or grieving clients, training seminars for requesting organizations, and public seminars at Kara.

Kara counselors commit themselves to one year of volunteer work, to a twenty-eight hour initial training workshop originated by the Kara staff and consultants and further developed by the author, and to a weekly support group and training session. Kara volunteers have given more than 50,000 hours since the program was established in 1976, currently serving about 200 people per month in sustained one-to-one relationships. Almost half of the volunteer counselors' hours have been devoted to their own training, reflecting Kara's strong emphasis on preparation for and support while doing this kind of work.

While Kara has learned from such pioneers in the field as Elisabeth Kübler-Ross and Charles Garfield, the counselors do not follow any one established approach. The Kara program has evolved from experience with clients. From this experience we have learned that, although loss and separation are universal, each person's experience is unique. Most people know, at some level, what is right for them; they need only support and affirmation in working through the complexities of an unfamiliar situation. Kara, therefore, does not provide specific answers, nor espouse a particular religion, discipline, or philosophy. Its counselors attempt instead to help people find their own personal path. The central goals are to decrease isolation by providing a personal connection and to enhance each client's sense of control and dignity.[2]

SOME OTHER TRAINING PROGRAMS

Other training workshops on the subject of death and grief are available. The two best known in the United States are those offered by Elisabeth Kübler-Ross and by Stephen Levine. Neither of these is oriented solely to training people to work with the dying and grieving, although students certainly will learn much in these courses that would serve this purpose.

Dr. Kübler-Ross, who wrote *On Death and Dying* in 1969, inspired the current surge of interest in death and grief.[3] Based on her work with dying patients, their physicians and nurses, clergy, and family members, she developed the *Life, Death, and Transition Workshops* that are now held all over the world. Structured as live-in five-day retreats, these workshops also help participants to get in touch with their long-repressed feelings and to recognize and deal with their own "unfinished business." Kübler-Ross believes that unconditional parental love and firm consistent discipline can create whole human beings, but as most of us have had little of these, we are full of fears, insecurities, resentments, and unshed tears. In her workshops she helps people to express and work through these blocks to a more full and harmonious life. She also teaches participants to accept death as an integral part of life and to maintain awareness of the finiteness of human existence.

Dr. Kübler-Ross is accompanied by trained assistants at every workshop, who help when a participant needs individual attention. She trains her assistants in the "externalization process" through a mixture of didactic information and work with their own emotional material. She believes that a person cannot work effectively with the dying and grieving without a regular release of his or her own emotional negativity and blocks to experience. Her assistants also receive ongoing training by watching her work with workshop participants.

Stephen Levine used to work with Dr. Kübler-Ross, but began to offer his own training sessions as he integrated the practice of Vipassanna meditation and Buddhist teachings into his work. He also founded a Dying Center in Taos, New Mexico, for people who are terminally ill. His book, *Who Dies?*, encourages individuals to use the awareness of death for the purpose of self-actualization.[4] He believes that we can die consciously only if we have lived consciously, and so supports a lifestyle of focused attention, meditation, and exploration of the self. Levine begins his workshop by asking participants to experience it as if they will die the moment it is over. The awareness of death is a strong theme that arouses participants and alters their sense of reality. Like Kübler-Ross, he perceives death as one of many transitions in existence, but he uses the imagery of the *Tibetan Book of the Dead* and other spiritual resources to guide individuals through transition.

Levine's workshop goal is twofold: He teaches participants to enrich their lives by practicing identification with the universe rather than their own bodies; and he reduces the anxiety surrounding death by increasing understanding of transcendance. Levine does not encourage emotional catharsis in the same way Kübler-Ross does. He supports personal sharing and emotional expression, but does not stress externalization. The participant expresses only those emotions that arise naturally in the workshop.

The trainings offered by both Kübler-Ross and Levine are powerful experiences, enabling participants to look anew at their relationship with death, and thus with life. These two programs differ from each other, as well as from Kara training, and people may find that one approach suits them better than another.

Hospice programs are being developed throughout the United States, and each has its own training program to meet its specific needs. Hospices primarily provide medical care and are based on a medical model. Kara is based on a psychological model, and focuses only on the emotional support aspect of the work. Kara is the emotional support component of two local hospices, and has provided training at several other hospices in counseling skills and personal death awareness. The information in this book should prove useful in hospice trainings and to hospice nurses.

KARA COUNSELING COMPARED TO PSYCHOTHERAPY

Counseling dying or grieving people is a specialized part of therapy. It involves different goals and often uses a different process of interaction. Often a lay person can provide the needed support. It is not usually appropriate to work directly on any psychopathology a counselor may encounter in a dying or grieving client. This is a time for healing, not uncovering work. Nonetheless, the lay counselor should be able to recognize unhealthy mental or emotional conditions and be prepared to refer clients to the appropriate professional for treatment.

Grief counseling has become necessary in this culture due to the breakdown of more traditional community or family support. J. William Worden describes the goals of grief counseling as facilitating completion of the mourning process. That is, the grief counselor needs to support the client in acknowledging his loss, expressing his pain and other emotions, readjusting to new roles and responsibilities, and finally, over a period of time, learning to understand the value of refocusing and connecting with others who may fill the empty space. Sometimes the mourning process is more complicated than this. Complications can arise from the absence of grief, delayed grief, or chronic grief. When this occurs, more chronic emotional states may be involved and the attention of a trained psychotherapist may be required[5]. J. William Worden recently wrote a valuable book, *Grief Counseling and Grief Therapy* that describes interventions for therapists involved in treating more complex grieving.[6]

The goals in counseling the dying are different from the usual psychotherapeutic goals. Some describe the goal of counseling as providing support and comfort. Others see resolution of fear and guilt as the ideal outcome. And still others believe self-actualization and a deeper understanding of the universe to be the goal. This author supports the goal that Avery Weisman described as helping people to die an "appropriate death"—that is, to die in a way that the individual client defines as dignified and acceptable.[7]

There are several other differences between counseling the dying and more traditional therapy. Rather than increasing discomfort, as is sometimes necessary in traditional psychotherapy, the goal usually is to increase comfort—psychologically, physically, and socially. The roles are different too; there is more informality between the dying patient and the counselor. The process of work may contain elements of psychotherapy, but it also is characterized by simple conversation, silence, and mutual sharing. There may be more stress on the completion of unfinished business and movement through the negative reactions to death to a state of acceptance if the client wants this. There is often an inherent incompleteness and lack of closure. All of life's problems will not be resolved. The focus is usually on process rather than accomplishment, and the patient is in charge of what is talked about and how. Finally, the counselor should encourage transference, which may be intense, but countertransference will result in his own bereavement, for which he will need the help of a good support group. In order to keep the relationship healthy, the counselor or therapist will need to have a place to release his own emotions.[8]

Those who counsel the dying need to examine their own attitudes about death and grief and to recognize that the patient or client knows best about his own experience. The counselor must also be trained to be empathic in the true sense of the word: paying attention, being present in the moment, and not losing a sense of himself as he identifies with the client's situation. To be empathic does not mean to be sympathetic; it is being connected while separate at the same time.

Counselors and caregivers to the dying and grieving need to know how to listen, to hear what the client is saying, to know their own personal reactions to what they hear, and to keep the two separate. A dying client needs to be respected for himself. The counselor must be able to tolerate ambivalence, uncertainty, and pain without needing to change or solve the "problem." Inherent in both dying and grieving is the act of facing the inevitable with integrity.

WHAT MAKES A GOOD CAREGIVER TO THE DYING?

Trainees at Kara often wonder whether they are suited to this kind of work and what problems they may encounter. The caregiver to the dying, whether nurse, hospice worker, mental health professional, friend or relative, is involved in a relationship that guarantees an ending. Every human connection, of course, must have an ending, but this is especially obvious to those who work with people who know their time on earth is limited. The counselor or caregiver has a commitment to make a connection with the patient or client, while knowing it will soon end. His or her own past experience with relationships—and especially with endings—and with loss, pain, and intimacy will color the relationship with clients.

Several important sources of resistance may block a counselor's attempt to connect with a dying client.[9] He may fear the burden of a client's dependency, the prospect of facing too much pain, or even his own inability to help. Such fears can prevent a counselor or caregiver from opening up or giving freely to a dying client.

"Shoulds" are another common block. New counselors, especially, may act out their ideal of the helping role rather than being authentically themselves. The desire to please creates another barrier to an honest and constructive relationship. The counselor or caregiver who tries to ingratiate the client by agreeing too readily or giving in to excessive demands does more harm than good. An effective counselor maintains his or her own identity and separateness, providing a strong basis for genuine relationship with the client.

An excessive need to be in control can also create a block. The counselor who is afraid to be vulnerable or open to new experience will not make a deep connection with clients. His willingness to face the unknown is particularly essential in working with the dying and grieving.

What makes an effective counselor? Those who work with the dying and grieving must be willing to reveal themselves without anticipating judgment and to allow others to do the same. The effective counselor will not identify so closely with the client that he or she may either become controlled by the relationship or try to control it. Counselors must not come to feel that separation (i.e., death) will mean the loss of a part of themselves. They must also be able to view disagreement as a statement of boundaries between individuals, not as a judgment of anyone's worth. It is possible to maintain an empathic relationship even with many differences, and a recognition of boundaries is a necessary ingredient of mutual respect.

Effective counselors also must be willing to work through their own problems or emotional reactions as they arise, not necessarily with the client, but with members of their support community. They must be committed to giving all they can to the client within a designated time and place, without hurting themselves or going against their own principles and personal inclinations. Perhaps most important of all, counselors or caregivers to the dying must be able to accept the fact that the "problem" is unsolvable. They must be able to simply *be with a client*, to give support and express concern and caring without giving in to the commonly felt need to *do something* about the unsolvable problem of terminal illness and impending death. This is the hardest task for many new counselors, but it can be learned through practice.

USING THIS BOOK

This volume, like the Kara program, embraces both the psychological and the spiritual or philosophical aspects of death and dying and of work with the dying and grieving. As such it blends the varied contributions of many others in this field. Part I of the book (Chapters Two through Four) provides a review of the information needed to do this kind of work. The many references to the work of others are intended both to provide a basic overview and to guide readers wishing to delve more deeply into this growing field. The material in Part I is presented to all the counselor trainees in the Kara program, and should be read and absorbed before moving on to the exercises in Part II.

Part II (Chapters Five through Eight) presents information and exercises in several different skill areas: attention; listening and responding; avoiding burnout; and personal exploration of death and grief. Learning to pay deep attention is the basis for any counseling, but combined with responding skills, it is especially important when working with the dying who may only want to receive silent attention. It is also essential, in order to prevent burnout, that caregivers have a place to express their own emotional stress and reactions to the pain. The personal exploration of death and grief chapter helps the reader to further understand how his feelings about death influence his living and his work with others. The exercises in this section may be completed before or after those relating to attention and listening and responding skills. A questionnaire, based on the work of Worden and Proctor, is used at Kara for self-exploration of personal attitudes and feelings about death and dying. It comes from their book, *PDA-Personal Death Awareness,* and may be used to supplement the exercises in this chapter.[10] Some of the other exercises used at Kara for personal death awareness training have been omitted from this volume as more appropriate for use in groups led by a skilled trainer (the entire series of exercises appears in the Trainers' Manual).

This book provides introductory training for people who work, or plan to work, with the dying and grieving. As a basic introduction to the field, the volume does not cover all aspects of this kind of work. It does not, for example, deal with family dynamics in times of stress, but emphasizes individual counseling. It does not address the special case of family grief in cases of suicide. Euthanasia and ethics are not covered. And, most important, the book does not attempt to present psychotherapeutic techniques in treating people with evident pathology. Psychotherapy, of course, involves advanced professional training. For those interested in pursuing related topics more deeply a bibliography is provided.

REFERENCES

[1] Henri Nouwen, *Out of Solitude*. Notre Dame, Ind.: Ave Maria Press, 1974, p. 34.

[2] I am indebted to Carol Lillibridge, Executive Director of Kara, who developed the written Kara philosophy after seven years in the agency.
    Kara was founded in 1976 by about twenty persons who saw a need for emotional support for community members facing life threatening illness or grief. The three incorporators are Theresa Wells, M.D.; Nancy Chilton, M.A.; and Martha Geiken Clayton. Kara is located at 457 Kingsley Ave., Palo Alto, Ca. 94301.

[3] Elisabeth Kübler-Ross, *On Death and Dying*. New York: Macmillan, 1969.

[4] Stephen Levine, *Who Dies?* Garden City, N.Y.: Anchor Press/Doubleday, 1982.

[5] J. William Worden, *Grief Counseling and Grief Therapy*, New York: Springer, 1982.

[6] *Ibid.*

[7] Avery Weisman, *On Dying and Denying*. New York: Behavioral Publications, 1972.

[8] E.S. Schneidman, "Some Aspects of Psychotherapy with Dying Patients," In: C. Garfield, *Psychosocial Care of the Dying Patient*. New York: McGraw-Hill, 1978.

[9] S. Luthman describes blocks to connection in any relationship and ways of overcoming them in *Intimacy: the Essence of Male and Female*. San Rafael, Calif.: Mehetabel, 1972.

[10] J. William Worden and W. Proctor, *PDA-Personal Death Awareness*. Englewood Cliffs, N.J.: Prentice Hall, 1976.

CHAPTER TWO

THE DEVELOPMENTAL
AWARENESS OF DEATH

*"When I meet new people they ask me
how many children I have. If I tell them I
have three children, then it naturally leads
into me telling them two have died, and the
new friend gets uncomfortable. But, if I tell
them I have one child, I feel that I have
betrayed the children I have lost."*
    — *Mother who lost an eight and
       ten year old in a plane crash*

Although affected by the teaching and rituals of our culture, our basic concepts of and feelings about death change over the course of our lifetime. Different approaches are appropriate with different age groups, as awareness of death tends to change with developmental changes in the individual. It is important for counselors of the dying or grieving to pay attention to the client's conception of death and grief. This chapter will give counselors insight into the resistances they may encounter and suggest what approach to take and what language to use in working with a particular client.

The brief descriptions of developmental stages provided here are intended to orient the reader to the *general* traits and tasks of each age group. It is important to remember that individuals go through these stages at different ages, although the sequence of stages may be the same. The stages also overlap and include previous stages. An adult may be operating at any or all stages at a given time. Particularly when under extreme stress, there may be some regression to earlier developmental stages. An adult in crisis often temporarily reverts to more primitive modes of operation and expression.

THE CHILD'S EXPERIENCE OF DEATH

Kara counselors have described memories of their reactions to the death of a family member when they were children. Most remember a calm matter-of-fact reaction if they experienced a loss through death before the age of seven. One woman told of her best friend's death when both were six years old. She recalled missing her friend very much, but even though she had no formal religious training, she said that she knew her friend was all right in "heaven." Her main concern had been that her friend would remain age six while she herself would grow older; when she died at 60 or more years of age they would not be able to play together.

Another Kara counselor recalled that when her father came to tell her and her sister that their grandfather had died they immediately decided that the grandfather must be in the room then, and both called out "Bye-bye, grandpa!" This woman remembered no tears or fear; the most difficult part of the experience had been the absence of her mother during the grandfather's illness and death.

The experiences of these two women are not uncommon. Young

children often are quite matter-of-fact about death and dying. Yet the experience is still a powerful one. Though not unpleasant, the memories of early childhood loss are often clear, detailed, and vivid.

During the period from birth to age two, the child relates to the world through touch, smell, taste, and vision.[1] If a child is dying or ill, or loses his mother at this time, his primary need will be for essential attachment behaviors. Bowlby describes the five attachment behaviors that console a child.[2] (These apply to teens and adults as well, since one never drops the behaviors of a previous stage. New behaviors are added on, but earlier ones—though latent—remain in a person's repertoire.)

The first attachment behavior is eye contact, one of the most powerful signs of connection available to us. The second attachment behavior is facial expression, usually smiling. The smile is one of the first expressions that the child observes in his parents as they let him know they love and recognize him. Dying children and other patients are often deprived of eye contact and of smiling, as caretakers may deliberately maintain a "stone face" to protect the child from emotion.

The third essential attachment behavior is touch. Birth centers often encourage the father as well as the mother of a newborn to have skin-to-skin contact immediately after birth to encourage bonding. Again, a sick child or adult may be deprived of this contact. In fact, in a hospital, touching may be associated with the negative experience of shots or the checking of vital signs.

The fourth attachment behavior is vocalization. In infancy this means crying and laughing. Music and singing also are a kind of connection.

The fifth consoling attachment behavior is feeding. Feeding should be a shared experience. A sign of nurturance and life, it should not be forced or hurried. The best way to feed a dying or grieving child is to eat with him and to use the experience to make contact.

All of these attachment behaviors are pre-symbolic, body-oriented, and essential for the child from birth to two years. Clearly also, they are essential for anyone at any age who is in great pain and needs primary-level comforting. For example, an eighteen year old boy dying of cancer in a hospital intensive care unit was very agitated and could not be calmed by anyone. Finally the music therapist persuaded a flute-playing street musician to come in and sit with him. In a short while, the patient's vital signs evened out and he and the rest of the unit calmed down.[3]

It is only after language develops that the child is capable of symbolic imagery.[4] At this point, from age two to five or seven, the child experiences life through his body and his mental capacities. It is at this time that he develops the ability to know something exists when he does not see or hear it. This is important for an understanding of the child's relationship with death. At this stage the child feels that the world revolves around him. He cannot understand that people exist independent of him or his wishes.

> They [children] have a hard time conceiving that anyone can have an independent existence, or have an independent will, or, most importantly, not be concerned with them at all . . . I think most of us operate at this level most of the time in our waking lives.[5]

This is the period when there is little distinction between what is alive or dead and what is imaginary or real. Imaginary friends are common. It is a time of ritual and make-believe. The child considers death to be like sleep (the most familiar way to experience the unconscious state), and he considers it reversible. There is a magical quality about it, and it is often accepted with calmness and ease. Up to this point the child has believed that he is invulnerable, with total control over the world. He considers himself special, and he expects a personal rescuer to save him from pain and death. Discussing the recent loss of his sister with his Kara counselor, a nine year old confided that at age five he believed that, although everyone else dies, he was special and would live forever.

Perhaps because he feels in control, a child at this stage may feel that his own illness or that of his relatives is his fault. Sickness may be considered a punishment for something he has done wrong. It is impossible for the young child to understand that death is irreversible, that the person who has died cannot come back if he wants to. The child may feel guilty, or he may be angry at the dead person for choosing not to return. If a parent or sibling dies when the child is at this age, he may regress to the pre-symbolic stage, needing touch and continual reassurance that others close to him will not disappear.

The main challenge in working with a child of this age is to help him to come to terms with his sense of responsibility for the death. He will need to use ritual, play, and fantasy in this process. It is useless to try to convince him with words that it is not his fault. This can be done later when he has more developed concrete thinking. What he needs now is support in expressing any feelings of anger at being deserted or sorrow at having done something "wrong." The child also needs to pay his respects to the dead. He can do this symbolically (as with a doll) or in fact (by attending the funeral). The child should be offered choices at this time, and respected for what he decides.

Somewhere between the ages of five and seven there is a developmental shift, documented cross-culturally, that marks a change in the child's capacity to think and understand.[6] This stage is a shifting from internal growth and make-believe to a readiness to relate to and understand the environment. After this shift occurs the child begins to understand space and time and to express a need for concrete facts. This stage usually lasts until the onset of puberty.[7] The child can now understand past, present, and future as he learns about his physical and social world. He wants to take things apart to learn how they work. He may begin collecting things. If a child at this age is dying, he wants to know everything he can about his treatment, and he often becomes an expert on some aspects of it.

> [Children of this age group] ... are really concrete operators, and they have huge amounts on their minds; about the treatment, the disease, and the environment where they are being treated. They become real sweethearts of the people who treat them. That is because they know everybody's name, everybody's history, and they relate to people as an extended family.[8]

When talking about death or grief the child wants to know specific facts. He needs to know the truth about his condition or that of a dying family member. The child can make better sense of his world if he is given this information, so it is important to respect his needs and requests.

A child begins to perceive death as adults know it at about the age of nine or ten. It is about this time that knowledge that he will die may become a conscious reality. Death becomes personally and universally inevitable. For the first time the child understands that he is not to be spared. If this new knowledge is accompanied by the onset of illness or the loss of a parent or sibling, there may be a great deal of fear as he grapples with the inevitable. It is important for the child of this age to attend the funeral of a loved one if he wishes to, as this will provide concrete evidence of the death.

There may also be a taunting of death or joking about it to alleviate the fear.[9] Some children counseled at Kara report being teased by their peers, and it is important to keep this in mind when working with children of this age group. School children wrote the following in a class on death:

> If you get shot
> You might rot.
>
> If you get strangled
> You might look mangled.

I hope I don't die till I'm old
So I won't mold.

When I die bury me deep
Plant some roses at my feet
Around my head the maggots will creep
It won't bother me, I'll be asleep!

I like death, death likes me
Oh, my gosh, my golly gee!
Death is nice, nicer than spice
It's the way we're meant to be!

If you think failing's bad
Wait till you die, that's pretty sad!

Don't think of life as a cheap shot
Think of it so it will mean a lot.[10]

    Children of this age group also can be sensitive and caring when faced with death and grieving. When two children aged nine and twelve were killed in an accident, their teachers arranged for their school-mates to build a memorial garden. The sixth-graders researched the costs and designed the garden, and the third-graders helped to dig up the earth and plant flowers. They also drew pictures for the family of the dead children and held a memorial service in the new garden, singing songs and talking about the children who had died. The whole process took about six months, from January to June, allowing for much discussion about death and birth and life, about beginnings and endings, about heaven and hell. The teachers observed that those children who had lost siblings or parents seemed to have especially vivid conceptions of what happens after death, and that in some instances the belief in heaven was a way to keep the world of make-believe and the idea of immortality alive.

    Pre-adolescents seem to recognize the concreteness of death through spontaneous flashes of insight that may or may not remain conscious.[11] Moments of understanding will be followed by actions that imply that the child is still using magical thinking. Adults, of course, also may react in this way. The important thing to remember, with adults or with children, is that the feelings a person is expressing at the moment are not the whole picture. Anyone under stress is likely to be experiencing a range of often conflicting emotions, and they should be allowed to express themselves freely.

A CASE STUDY

A young child may not talk directly about death. Art, play, and sand-tray work have all proven effective in communicating about death or grief with children between ages two and nine. At Kara, two children learned about and assimilated the fact of their mother's death in the following way.

Bobby was nine years old; his sister Ann was six. Their mother, in her early thirties, was dying of brain cancer. She was divorced from her husband, who had not lived in the same town for several years. The mother was uncertain about how to prepare her children for her death. The family cared deeply for each other. The children went to visit their mother daily in the hospital and were included in many aspects of her care and treatment. Yet the adults had difficulty talking to the children about the fact that their mother would die, and they felt that their mother should not discuss it with them.

The counselor, Jane, spent a lot of time playing with the children on the swings, coloring, and allowing that to lead naturally into talk about dreams and stories. Generally, the children did not speak directly about their mother. Then one day Bobby showed clearly how he was working through his mother's illness: he drew a huge octopus crushing him and the world. He described it as a dream he had had the night before. Some weeks before he had been told that his mother's tumor was growing "with tentacles" through her brain, and that was the reason the doctors could not operate.

Jane found a rhythm in being with the children. They seemed to relate to play as both an avoidance and an expression of their emotions. Often, after initial unfocused play, something significant would be expressed if Jane guided the discussion. She found that while this story-telling was effective, when something painful was touched upon, distractive behavior would often crop up. One time Ann asked Jane to "stop talking about Mommy or I'll cry." Jane reassured her by saying that it was all right to cry.

One day, a few weeks before the mother's death, the following conversation occurred:

Bobby: "Is my Mommy going to die?"

Jane: "Yes, she is."

Ann: "She is?"

Jane: "Yes."

Bobby: "You are the first person who told us that."

Jane: "What did the others tell you?"

Bobby: "That she *might* die."

They showed intense interest, almost excitement, over this. The neighbor looked over the fence, and Bobby announced in a clear unemotional tone, "My Mommy is going to die." The neighbor smiled uncertainly and moved quickly away.

Bobby: "Will she die tomorrow?"

Bobby then began to play on an outdoor gym doing back flips to the ground. After two of these flips, he asked for help, saying he was afraid. Jane supported him, and after one more, he told her he was "scared to death," afraid he would fall. He said he could not do any more flips. During this exchange, Ann sat with total concentration unraveling a heavy rope.

Walking together to the house, they met the children's grandmother.

Bobby: "Guess what? Mommy is going to die!"

All of them sat down, and questions poured forth from Bobby:

"Why did Mommy get cancer?"

"When is she going to die?"

"Why didn't chemotherapy work?"

"I wish Mommy could be home."

Ann talked about school, mimicking her classmates: how everyone would look at her with wide eyes, and at each other, when they find out. She was anxious about being stared at and laughed at if she cried.

Another relative entered the room, and the children announced that Mommy was going to die. She told them she knew already, and they were surprised. The conversation continued, interspersed with discussion of homework and the playground, Bobby doing tricks, and Ann playing with a necklace.

Finally Bobby said, "I have a funny feeling inside that Mommy is going to die." He immediately switched the subject and described his back flips to his grandmother. Jane was surprised at the sudden change in focus. But when he started describing the "funny feeling" he got when he did back flips, she put the two together, and asked if it felt the same as when he thought about his mother dying. He said yes. This is a clear indication that his back flips expressed his anxiety and were an effort to cope with his mother's death.

During this time, the children smiled often, were matter-of-fact, and shed no tears, and the counselor sensed some relief intermingled with anxiety. "It's good to know because I am preparing myself," said Bobby. There was a clear difference between Bobby and Ann in their coping styles. Bobby needed specific facts about the treatment and future, while Ann was expressive mostly through her play and magical stories. Yet this example shows how the growth stages are never distinct and separated, with Bobby especially interspersing symbolic play with concrete questions.

ADOLESCENCE AND DEATH

The adolescent struggle is permeated by intensity—the experience of life at its fullest. Adolescents are awakening both to sexuality and to death, and each new awareness enlarges the boundaries of the self, while at the same time causing some fear and anxiety over the new boundaries.

Adolescence is a process of extricating the self from a dependency on parents, of becoming an individual. It is also a time of much ambivalence. The more a person separates himself from others, the closer he comes to recognizing his own existential isolation.

Death imagery may intensify each time a person goes through a life transition. Adolescence itself is often a major anxiety-provoking transition. With the striking physical changes comes a new loss of control. The child develops new cognitive capacities, coming to recognize not only what is but also what might be, could have been, or should be.[12] This is when the child starts to ask the Big Why questions. Why is there suffering? Why am I here? Why does God allow pain? Why me? Why her?

A twelve year old was talking to a Kara counselor about his father's death when he was seven. He did not remember feeling much pain at the time; his concern had been for his mother, who fainted when she heard the news. Not until quite recently had he begun to grieve deeply and to ask questions about the loss of his father.

An adolescent anticipating the death of a family member may go through intense survivor guilt. When all the questions of meaning arise, the question "Why her and not me?" also comes up. There seems to be little a teenager can count on at such stressful times, so there is often regressive behavior. The adolescent may avoid the dying person or he may become a constant caregiver. Either behavior may be a reaction to guilt and confusion.

If a peer dies, and there is an opportunity for groups of teens to meet and discuss it, the counselor should take advantage of it. On several occasions Kara counselors have supported a community of teens grieving over the loss of a fellow student. It is a time of deep soul-searching, and there is a driving need to express (sometimes quite dramatically) the pain and shock of the loss. Teachers should be supported in holding discussion groups, or an ongoing grief group should be encouraged.

If a teenager himself is dying, he will be outraged at being robbed of his life, his potential wasted. With such feelings, he may be aggressive or withdrawn, but the counselor needs to respect and support his anger in either case by acknowledging his situation.[13] There are special problems for the dying adolescent. The teenage years are a time when the self is defined by group norms, and being ill sets him apart from his peers. The result is a loss of self-esteem and a magnification of the usual identity problems. This age group commonly copes by using defenses of denial and overcompensation, and the dying teenager may attempt to downplay his illness in order to seem normal or work especially hard at being accepted by his peers. Both of these defenses can serve the teen in his survival, and should not be denied him as long as he is not physically harmed.

Many adolescents use their intellect to analyze their emotions. They may ask many questions and want to read everything about their illness. It is usually appropriate to be honest and direct with the dying adolescent. The information they seek will give them a sense of control and provide a framework for understanding and explaining the situation. With the adolescent also, if the illness leads to physical changes there is a special shame and vulnerability about appearance that should be treated with care and sensitivity.

The death of a teenager is devastating. These are supposed to be the years of blossoming and of creation. The personality is taking shape and life is full of promise. There are few words to describe teens' and their parents' feelings of anger and loss when death in the teen years becomes inevitable. Ted Rosenthal, a student at the University of California, Berkeley, who was dying of leukemia, wrote the following poem, "How Could I Not Be Among You?" It speaks poignantly of the frustration, desperation, and powerlessness of dying, especially for a young person being robbed of so much of his life.

Though you may find me picking flowers
Or washing my body in the river, or kicking rocks,
Don't think my eyes don't hold yours.
And look hard upon them
And drop tears as long as you stay before me
Because I live as a man who knows death
And I speak only the truth
To those who will listen.
Never yield a minute to despair, sloth, fantasy.
I say to you, you will face pain in your life
You may lose your limbs, bleed to death
Shriek for hours or into weeks in unimaginable agony.
It is not aimed at anyone
But it will come your way,
The wind sweeps over everyone ...
Step lightly, we're walking home now.
The clouds take every shape.
We climb up the boulders; there is no plateau.
We cross the stream and walk up the slope.
See, the hawk is diving.
The plain stretches out ahead, then the hills, the valleys, the meadows.
Keep moving people. How could I not be among you?[14]

ADULTHOOD AND DEATH

The struggles adults experience in relation to death are different from those of children. Life no longer holds unlimited possibilities. Choices have been made, directions taken, and there is some urgency about time and its limitations. Adults are more likely to worry over "wrong" decisions and to regret the lack of time to make amends. For the fully developed adult, however, this can be a time of creativity and growing enlightenment, of affirming the sense of self and dropping any unnecessary layers.

Middle age is definitely a time for recognizing that some of the doors of life are no longer open. One may die before achieving the feeling that everything is complete. "The youth 'knows about' death; the older adult is more likely to sense death as an intimate companion ... an intimacy that increases with the years."[15]

Middle age is a time when acquaintances, friends, and family begin to die. Grief usually is no longer a stranger. Yet loss of parents, even when expected, may make a person feel suddenly orphaned or the "next in line." Grief is felt not only for the dead, but for the survivors as well. A fifty-five year old woman who lost her grandson and then her son, both in accidents only a year and a half apart, kept repeating that "it's all backwards." She was supposed to die first. Losing her son was like losing her future, and she could hardly bear the pain—let alone reconfirm her own will to live and move on. The meaning of her life had been abruptly taken away, and she needed to find new meaning in the midst of her pain.

The acutely grieving adult may regress to sensory, symbolic, concrete or teenage levels of operating. He may need nonverbal eye contact, touch, and comforting. He may need to find a new source of the basic attachment behaviors he experienced with the person who has died. The emptiness will eventually be filled only by other attachments.

On a symbolic level, the grieving adult often uses ritual and fantasy in an attempt to get the dead person back. A part of him may feel responsible for the death and personally punished for something he did wrong. There was a man who was ice fishing in New England in the winter with his son. The child fell through the ice and drowned. He dove in and tried to find the boy, but the body was never recovered. It was after fifteen years of psychoanalysis that he realized why he had taken up scuba diving, and had been a scuba diver for years. As soon as he realized that he was looking for his lost son, he never went into the water again.[16]

The adult also will feel the emotions of anger, betrayal, sorrow, and guilt. When an adult is functioning at this level, it is as pointless to talk him out of his sense of responsibility as it would be in the case of a child. He has to express it and work it through on the symbolic level, pay his respects, try to understand, experience his misgivings, and express his anger to the dead.

The concrete level of functioning surfaces when the adult needs to know exactly what happened at the death, what could have been done, and who did what. He needs to know every detail, to obtain every concrete reminder he can of the person's last days or hours. In the case of a stillborn child, anything that can show the parent that the child was alive is important. Cuttings of hair, fingernails, a picture, footprints should be saved for the parents.[17] This will help the parents fill their need for concrete information, and will help them recognize that the life and death did occur. The grieving process is much more difficult if the body is not seen or recovered, and the grieving adult will have a hard time believing the reality of the death if there is no evidence of it.

Finally, the teenage operational level is in evidence when the bereaved adult questions God and fate and rages at the loss: "Why him?" "Why me?" This question is the most difficult one that a counselor will have to confront. There is no satisfactory answer. The counselor can only let the bereaved know that he recognizes the pain, the sense of betrayal, and the disbelief.

When an adult is coping in the sensory or symbolic mode, it is pointless to discuss the matter rationally. It would be more appropriate to provide eye contact, touch, or respond symbolically. An example of this was given by a Kara client who found she had cancer. Her friends immediately wanted to "help" her by effecting a change in her attitude toward the illness so she would not feel victimized. She raged at them to leave her alone, stating that she had no interest in changing her attitude. All she wanted was to hurt and be comforted. Months later, she herself initiated a process of looking at how she could help herself by thinking differently about her illness. It was a matter of timing, understanding, and careful attention.

When facing serious illness in a child, parents not only feel shock and disbelief, but also a sense of guilt and responsibility that can be partly based on fact. The guilt can come from not having recognized the symptoms early enough or from not having done enough or appreciated the child enough before he was sick. Other issues that may come up concern how much to tell the child, what to do with siblings, how to adjust to the doctor making decisions for the child, and how to bear the child's pain or suffering as well as their own. Many parents find it intolerable to consider their child's death as a meaningless turn of fate and create some medical or spiritual reason for the illness to help alleviate their self-blame and the feeling that they have somehow failed.

Many marriages are threatened after the loss of a child. It is well known among people who work with seriously ill children that divorce is not an unusual aftermath to a child's death. This may happen because the husband and wife have different emotional responses, styles of caring for the ill child, or different styles of grieving after the child has died. When their styles are similar, they can derive much comfort from each other. But there isn't much room for comforting when their styles are not similar and both feel raw, isolated, drained, and needy. Of course, any pre-existing marital troubles may be compounded by the loss.

If the child was killed in an accident or died suddenly, guilt and feelings of responsibility may be especially intense. Marriage partners may blame each other as well as themselves, and competent counseling is usually essential for both.

Chapter Three will discuss in more detail the adult's experience of dying and grieving.

OLD AGE AND DEATH

When a person reaches old age, he probably has already grieved over many deaths. Time takes on a new dimension. Priorities change. The elderly may reminisce as a way of reassuring themselves that their lives have had meaning. Values are redefined and the relationship with the body changes.[18] The longer a person lives, the more likely he is to outlive his friends and close relations. Loneliness intensifies, and childhood anxieties about dependency and separation are reawakened. The contradictory feelings of not wanting to be a burden while at the same time not wanting to be abandoned begin to trouble him.

Erik Erickson describes two conflicts that adults experience in the second half of life. These are generativity versus stagnation and integrity versus despair.[19] In contrast to the seeming endlessness of life and the apparently unlimited choices one experiences as a youth, the older adult experiences finiteness and a greater need for meaning in the here and now. Along with this clearer sense of reality and of the present, there is a greater possibility of despair about unfulfilled dreams. But the older adult can also turn this possibility for despair into a sense of freedom. When agendas shift from long-range planning to more immediate concerns, there is a potential for greater simplicity and a lessening of responsibility. A seventy-eight year old man dying of cancer told his Kara counselor: "I'm not afraid to die. I've lived a long, full life, and I've had two wonderful wives, friends, the church, God. I'm lucky."

Studies have shown that fear of death tends to decrease with age, not only in our culture but in others as well.[20] This lessening of fear may come from a disengagement with life as families and friends die. The need to cope with grief repeatedly may help people to work through their relationship with death. Physical illness may set in and the future becomes less attractive. Or seventy to seventy-five years may be seen as the normal life-span, and to die around that time may seem to be the inevitable measure.[21] The elderly do think about death more than the young, and they often are better prepared for it. But not all go as peacefully as the man described above, and counselors will encounter some elderly people who face death with as much fear and frustration as any much younger person.

This brief description of the developmental awareness of death should give counselors and caregivers a basic understanding of the different ways in which children, adolescents, adults, and the elderly may react to their own impending death or the death of someone close to them. The point to remember is that one's relationship to death changes over the course of a lifetime, but that earlier ways of relating are not necessarily outgrown. Anyone may revert temporarily to more primitive stages in a time of crisis.

We will turn now to the subject of grieving, the different kinds and stages of grief, and the reactions of the dying person and of those around him to the fact of death and dying.

REFERENCES

[1]The stages of development described here are based primarily on Piaget. See: Herbert Ginsberg and Sylvia Opper, *Piaget's Theory of Intellectual Development: An Introduction*, Englewood Cliffs, N.J.: Prentice-Hall, 1969.

[2]John Bowlby, *Attachment and Loss* (Vol. 2): *Separation*, New York: Basic Books, 1969.

[3]Dr. John Golenski, lecture on child development, January 1983, at Kara, Palo Alto, California.

[4]*Supra* note 1.

[5]*Supra* note 3.

[6]Ibid. Also see: J. Choran, *Modern Man and Morality*, New York: Macmillan, 1964; I. Yalom, *Existential Psychotherapy*, New York: Basic Books, 1980; R. Kastenbaum and R. Aisenberg, *The Psychology of Death*, New York: Springer, 1972; M. Nagy, "The Child's Theories Concerning Death," in S. Wilcox and M. Sutton, *Understanding Death and Dying*, Palo Alto, Calif.: Mayfield Publications, 1981.

[7]*Supra* note 3.

[8]*Ibid.*

[9]Yalom, *supra* note 6.

[10]F. Sternberg and B. Sternberg, *If I Die and When I Do*, Englewood Cliffs, N.J.: Prentice-Hall, 1980, p. 79.

[11]R. Kastenbaum, "Death and Development Through the Lifespan," in H. Feifel (ed.), *New Meanings of Death*, New York: McGraw-Hill, 1977, p. 36.

[12]*Supra* note 3.

[13] *Ibid.*

[14] T. Rosenthal, *How Could I Not Be Among You?* New York: Persea Books, 1973, p. 79-80, 89.

[15] *Supra* note 11.

[16] *Supra* note 3.

[17] *Ibid.*

[18] R.J. Lifton and E. Olson, *Living and Dying,* New York: Praeger, 1974.

[19] Erick Erickson, *Childhood and Society* (2nd ed.), New York: Norton, 1963.

[20] R. Kalish, *Death, Grief, and Caring Relationships,* Monterey, Calif.: Brooks-Cole, 1981.

[21] *Ibid.*

CHAPTER THREE

GRIEFWORK

"I remember when my grandfather died. My grandmother was crying a lot. People were saying don't cry—pull yourself together. One day, when we were sitting on the couch, she started to cry. She apologized to me. She said, 'I'm sorry I'm crying.' She started telling me how she feels terrible because it's hard for everyone when she cries. She tries not to cry during the day, but at night when she goes to bed she cries into her pillow all night. She had lived with my grandfather so many years . . . Knew him when she was just a little girl. And they had been close for years and years. I think that experience really made me feel that there has got to be a place for people where it's alright for them to grieve and it's OK for them to have their feelings."

—Kara multimedia
presentation, 1980

Grief, or bereavement, is a reaction to the experience of loss. Any type of loss may be involved, not just the death of another person. Simos divides the experience of loss into four categories: developmental loss, loss of external objects, loss of parts of the self, and loss of a significant person.[1]

Developmental loss. The sense of loss begins at birth with the first separation from the mother. Separation occurs again with the loss of the mother's breast and with toilet training. Then, as the child grows, the birth of other siblings insures the loss of his original position in the family. The adolescent experiences loss of childhood as he moves through puberty. Each developmental loss brings with it new challenges and a new identity or role, but there is often an accompanying temporary loss of self-esteem as each adjustment is made.[2] Each stage involves grief of some kind, and each helps to lay the groundwork for our lifelong reactions to grief.

Loss of external objects. The first objects lost could be the child's favorite basket or toy. Moving from one house or neighborhood to another can also elicit childhood grief. Changing from one grade in school to another marks a transition for the child. As adults, losing a purse or wallet may stimulate an emotional reaction of grief as well as anger at having to replace lost items.

Loss of parts of self. Our relationship to the loss of parts of the self has developmental origins, beginning with the infant's development of body image. Any major change in a person's understanding of his own identity may elicit a grief reaction. Of course, any loss of the physical or functioning parts of the body always involves mourning and the realization that aging cannot be stopped.

Aging implicitly involves grief. Worsening eyesight or back trouble may be the first signs of age. Loss of memory, the ability to make decisions, or the control of body functions, and loss of independence are all signs of the inevitable loss of our bodies.

Grieving one's own impending death is similar to grieving the death of a loved one. The content is different, but the process may be the same.

Loss of a significant person. Every act of love brings with it a potential grief of separation. Separations range from short good-byes to the ending of the relationship through either a decision to leave or death. Loss of a loved one is one of the most painful experiences a person is likely to suffer.

What is important to recognize is that loss and grief patterns are ongoing and cumulative. Each loss can reawaken past losses. As our lives progress, we develop an individual pattern for living with loss. How we adjusted to loss as children and the nature of our losses in youth will determine how we grieve in adulthood.

In this chapter we are considering the entire continuum of grief over the loss of a significant person, from recognizing that death is imminent to post-death grief. There are common elements in the anticipatory grief of family and friends and that of the dying patient. The path diverges when the patient starts on the dying trajectory and the caregiver begins to anticipate life after the death of a loved one.

Of course, if there is no illness before death, the anticipatory grief and dying process are missing or vastly altered. Generally speaking, less anticipatory grief means a more intense grief after death.

The following section is intended to orient the reader to the patient's or family's experience of grief. Reference will be made to the counselor's role, but it is important to note that there is no way to work with the dying or grieving "by the book." The caregiver must maintain the sensitivity and presence to allow a trusting and fluid relationship to develop and understand that it is vital that each person do or be exactly what he feels is needed at the moment.

I. ANTICIPATORY GRIEF

Anticipatory grief allows the dying patient and his family to prepare for the fact of death. The period of anticipatory grief is a time to conclude unfinished business and to prepare financially, practically, and emotionally for the death. When anticipatory grieving has successfully occurred, the shock phase of post-death grief may be reduced. In this phase crucial decisions need to be made, questions need to be answered, hope and despair emerge and retreat. The caregivers are often exhausted and under tremendous stress. Sometimes they consciously choose not to experience their emotions, but use all their energy taking care of the practical and survival needs of the patient and themselves. Even if it is not expressed, there is a common, well known pattern describing a person's reaction to impending loss.

Elisabeth Kübler-Ross defines the stages of reaction to loss, specifically anticipatory grief, as follows:

Denial and shock. This is usually the period immediately after one has been told that death may occur. Frequent responses are: "This can't be true." "I don't believe it." Often there is numbness.

Anger. Rage at God, the doctors, or anything for letting this happen is common. Helplessness may underline these outbursts.

Bargaining. There is often a return to childhood egocentricity. "There must be something I can do to right this wrong" is a common response.

Depression. The inevitability of the loss becomes more real. There is a profound grasp of the utter futility of the situation.

Acceptance. This may or may not occur in anticipatory grief. If it does, there is a noticeable decrease in inner turmoil and conflict.[3] These stages do not always appear in this order. Some may not appear at all, in fact. But this list can give the counselor a guideline for the general reactions he may encounter.

There are other ways of describing human adaptation to serious illness and impending death. Avery Weisman describes a process involving: recognition of the reality of the illness; rejecting the threatening parts of that reality; replacement of these parts with a more tolerable reality; and reorientation to the changes. This reorientation entails recognizing the reality of death and giving in to some aspects of the loss. Then the conflict may be resolved (with intermittent periods of denial) and the family may reorient itself to the changes the new reality implies. At this point, if reality means facing a terminal illness, the patient may begin to look at the fact of personal extinction and at the meaning of life.[4]

It is now well known that the stages of grieving are never clear-cut, may be simultaneous, often do not appear in the given order, and may not all be experienced by some people. Still, it is useful to recognize and understand the various stages a grieving person may go through, especially for the counselor who hopes to make the patient's or client's passage easier.

II. THE PATIENT'S EXPERIENCE OF DYING

"I am dying ... No one likes to talk about such things. In fact, no one likes to talk much at all ... I am the one who is dying. I know you feel insecure, don't know what to say, don't know what to do. But please believe me, if you care, you can't go wrong. Just admit that you care. This is what we search for. We may ask for whys and wherefores, but we really don't want answers. Don't run away. Wait. All I want to know is that there will be someone to hold my hand when I need it. I'm afraid ... I've never died before."[5]

—a 13 year old boy dying of leukemia,
quoted in Kalish, 1981.

The surviving family member or friend outlives the anticipatory stage in the grief process; but for the patient himself, this is the only time he has to respond to the fact of his death. The frustration felt by some is expressed in this observation by a dying Kara client: "It's just a mess! Who needs it? But that's what's playing in my life right now. I never really liked sad endings. I tend to walk out on movies if they get really grim. But this movie I can't walk out on."[6]

The goal of the counselor here is to help the dying person answer the questions and master the fears and anxieties that death may evoke. In doing so, the counselor must strike a balance between recognizing the themes common to all dying and grieving and responding to a particular client's individual needs for learning, growth, and mastery of his situation.

A person's beliefs about immortality deeply affect his fears of death and the process of his dying. Some prospective counselors have come to Kara saying that they were comfortable with death either because they had lost so many people in their lives already or because their spiritual perspective allowed them to see death as a beginning rather than an ending. This also has been true of some of our grieving or dying clients. But to many people death means entering the dark unknown, and to all it is an ending, even if it is considered a beginning as well.

E.M. Pattison constructed the diagram appearing as Figure 1. He maintains that the knowledge of imminent death precipitates an acute life crisis, and that the time between this knowledge and death itself is a time for successful or unsuccessful crisis intervention.[7] According to Pattison, there are three phases in the period of dying. The knowledge of imminent death initiates the acute crisis period, which ends in the peak of anxiety. After this there is a period of chronic living-dying, during which the patient successfully integrates the realization of his death or fails to do so. This period ends in the terminal phase just before the moment of death.

**FIGURE 1.
THE EXPERIENCE OF DYING***

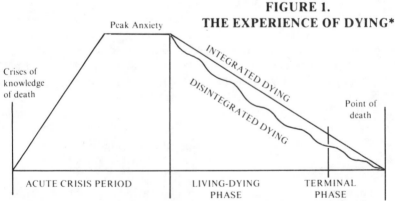

*Source: E.M. Pattison, *The Experience of Dying,* Englewood Cliffs, N.J.: Prentice-Hall, 1977, p.44.

THE ACUTE CRISIS PERIOD

No counselor can change the fact of death, but he or she can support the dying person in his crisis so that the living-dying phase does not lead to chaotic disintegration. The counselor also can help the patient adapt to the constant changes and losses entailed in dying, and to maintain dignity and self-respect as he follows his own unique path to death.

Pattison outlined five characteristics of the crisis of facing one's death, which can be summarized as follows:

1. The event poses a problem that is, by definition, insoluble. Stress is created or aggravated by the fact that the problem must simply be accepted.

2. The problem is beyond conventional problem-solving methods. The dying person is faced with a situation with which he has no prior experience.

3. The problem presents a direct threat to the person's life goals. Even in old age it interrupts a person in the midst of life.

4. As one faces the crisis of death, anxiety usually rises to a peak, during which the dying person either learns to cope or experiences disorganization and capitulates. Either way, anxiety then usually diminishes as one moves closer to death.

5. Dying reawakens dependency, identity, and other problems from the past; so in dying one is faced not only with the problem of death but with a host of unresolved problems from earlier in life.[8]

Pattison concludes that while the counselor cannot change the ultimate outcome of death, he can help the dying person look at the process of dying and help him to cope successfully with those aspects of it which he can control.

Feelings of numbness, paralysis, and denial may be part of the patient's initial reaction to the news of impending death. The counselor's primary task at this stage is to provide emotional support and to be a stable influence. He must not allow himself to become overwhelmed by the acute anxiety he sees in the patient.

THE LIVING-DYING PHASE

Once the person is labeled as dying, his relationship with himself as well as with his environment changes radically. He has certain tasks he may want to accomplish. The main ones are: completing unfinished business with others; participating in his own care and physical needs; adjusting to change and loss; arranging for what happens after he dies; and facing the fact of death itself.

The living-dying phase is one in which maximum interaction with the outside world is possible. In this phase also the individual may come to terms with the fact of his own mortality. As he does so a range of emotions are likely to surface—fear, denial, depression, anger, hope, and acceptance.

Fear may be the primary emotion as a person faces death. Some of the tangible forms that fear takes for the dying patient are fear of the unknown, fear of loss of control, fear of loneliness, fear of loss of family and friends, fear of loss of body, fear of loss of identity, fear of regression, and fear of emotional or physical pain.[9]

Fear of the Unknown

A person's relationship with the unknown influences most of his actions in life. It is usually subconscious, and its far-reaching effects go unrecognized. Facing impending death may stimulate a person to examine his beliefs about the nature of that unknown and impermanence itself. A person with a strong religious orientation may not spend much time thinking in this way, although the imminence of death may stimulate some to re-examine all of their spiritual beliefs.

Exploring the unknown often entails questioning the fundamental assumptions upon which one's life is based. It can lead to disintegration and loss of faith or to a renewed sense of life and of purpose, even for the dying person. The outcome of this relationship with the unknown is a big factor influencing the outcome of Kübler-Ross' stage of acceptance.

Freud believed that in the end, when facing death, a person has only three choices to help him find security. He can find shelter in religion (Freud strongly believed that religious ideas were based on illusion.) He can accept the ideas of religion, recognizing their mythical quality. Or he can rely upon reason to rationalize the threat of death.[10] As the following examples show, people who know they are dying may resort to all three. One Kara client wrote:

What is amazing to me is how a person can sit there and say that he realizes that he has no true knowledge of how he got here or when his life began, or of how anything was in the beginning (and in fact there may be no beginning), that the universe is infinite and what appears to be solid is actually millions of moving molecules. There are no real boundaries and time has nothing to do with what our clocks say. With this in mind, I wonder how a person can get up, get dressed, and go to work in the morning.

Life is like a drop of water appearing from some vast nowhere, absolutely without any visible base or foundation, and going nowhere—a brief glimpse of 'am-ness.' In light of this, not only can a person function, but in order to function he creates vast worlds of cause and effect relationships, seemingly solid senses of purpose, societies that follow rules and laws. It is extraordinary how we maintain the illusion of security and solidness in this flash of tangible time in the middle of such unknowableness.

I am at once in total awe of the human being and appreciate the sheer genius it takes to build such a phenomenally consistent system, especially when it is based on unknowing. How can we dare come up to the boundaries we have created and break them down? We might approach an intolerable truth. But in fact we are continually touching this truth and interpreting it however we wish.

I may have around me ways I know I'll live forever, a true sense of meaning for my life, and a belief in the eternal, but the question of the creation and death of my person, my body, my personality is difficult to tolerate for a long period of time.

Another client at Kara said:

When I was a young girl, I was lying in bed ready to go to sleep. This is a time when I was very close to myself, no outside distractions: a time to review the day.

I don't remember what led up to it, but I was thinking about dying. The words "I am going to die" kept repeating in my mind and suddenly I felt a shift.

The normal veil between me and that knowledge dropped, and knowledge became understanding. I felt deep inside the fear and panic that came from the understanding that one morning the sun will rise and I won't see it. This very body, this hand, these eyes, through which I experience so much beauty, will be gone. This I know is true.

No benevolent super-being or parent will save me.

I felt my mind reach out for something to save me, to reassure me that I was wrong. In my mind's eye, my arms grasped and clawed upward wanting to touch some different knowledge that could change this truth.

I started crying and ran to my sister's room for comfort.

This experience has happened to me repeatedly through my life since that night. The main thing it shows me is how thick the illusion is that I live in, in my daily life, to protect myself from this shock; and even when I've experienced that veil removed one hundred times, I still usually act as if I'm immortal.

A poignant example of grappling with the unknown was provided by another Kara client, a woman in her fifties who found out she had a brain tumor. She was paralyzed for a while, but with a course of chemotherapy, the tumor shrank, and she regained full movement. During this reprieve, she said she didn't think she could live if she got worse again.

Soon after, doctors found cancerous cells in her bones. They told her it was incurable. Her anguish and rage were uncontrollable. As she lost her hair from chemotherapy, she berated her counselor for being healthy. ("I'd like to take your head and put it through that wall.") She refused comfort or understanding, saying no one around really knew what it was like to be facing disintegration and the death sentence. All she was getting, she said, was condescension and denial from her friends.

She visualized death as total darkness. Her image was one of dirt being thrown onto a dark coffin underground.

As her panic escalated she began to make suicide threats. She did not want to die and knew it. The talk of suicide was a desperate attempt to control things, even if it meant facing the unknown abyss. The unknown itself seemed more acceptable than the torture of anticipating it.

The counselor's approach in this case was to encourage the woman to consider what could be structured and controlled in her life and to acknowledge the total helplessness they both felt about her impending death. This client also was referred to a psychiatrist for medication to help her to be in a state of mind to make these choices for herself.

For the counselor: When a client is questioning life's purpose or looking at the question of what comes after death, it is best to affirm the fear and be available for as much expression of it as possible. However, it is appropriate to try to balance this exploration with a look at the present situation in order to determine what the patient can control. A counselor can supply specific answers and concrete information. He or she can help the client distinguish between concerns about concrete issues over which some measure of control can be exercised and philosophical questions about the unknown that cannot be answered or controlled.[11]

Fear of Loss of Control

The ultimate loss of control occurs when life is taken away. There is no bargain that can be struck to avoid the ultimate end. This loss of control also occurs in a person grieving the loss of another.

Two primary issues are to be considered when the dying person is in crisis. One is the person's internal response to the inevitability of loss of control. This can lead to turmoil and rebellion, surrender, or reconciliation. The other issue involves identifying areas of care that can be controlled by the patient.

A client of Irvin Yalom had breast cancer that had spread to her brain.[12] She was warned that she would become paralyzed, but inwardly she believed she was special and that it wouldn't happen to her. When she did become paralyzed, she had to face the fact of the indifference of the universe. In her despair she struggled with the fact of her total impotence to help herself. "When it comes to aging and when it comes to dying," she said, "what I wish has absolutely nothing to do with it."[13] Yalom observes that accepting the fact of death includes recognizing our finiteness, our unimportance in the eyes of the universe, and our ultimate lack of control over how and when our life on earth will end.[14]

Dr. James Corby, a psychiatrist at Stanford University, is currently studying the factors that determine the quality of life for dying patients, using Kara clients and counselors for part of the study. From Dr. Corby's research it seems that the issue of control is a large one and is manifested in many ways. Clients feel the need to die in a familiar space with a minimum of new input, and to have control of their pain medication. Other control needs reflect each person's personality or social situation. The inevitable cannot be controlled. However, a person who is able to make some of the decisions affecting his daily life gains a sense of being in control of something, responsible for something.

For the counselor: Loss of control includes the loss of control of body functions, loss of control of decisions and events in the environment, loss of control of emotions, and the ultimate loss of control over the decision to live or die.

The counselor should help the client to exercise decision-making power in all possible areas. These range from wills and funeral arrangements to aspects of his own care. The client should determine, to the best of his ability, how he wants to live this last part of his life both psychologically and physically. Loss of control then can be a gradual

55

process, with the client feeling that his personal integrity is supported along the way.

Fear of Loneliness and Isolation

When a person takes time to sit alone without distraction, he may uncover a sense of how alone he really is. This may begin with the recognition that each of us will die alone no matter who else is present. Recognition of our ultimate aloneness may begin with facing an illness or making major life decisions. Despite our capacity for intimacy, our spiritual sense of oneness, or how connected with ourselves we may feel, there is an isolation that naturally occurs during dying and grief.

The isolation of dying is compounded by the way in which dying people are managed. The hospital usually is not geared to the care of the dying; it is oriented to curing. Until the hospice movement is more fully accepted, and dying people are supported in their own social environments, dying will continue to be a time of extreme loneliness and isolation.

There may always be some social isolation of the terminally ill, since withdrawal from normal routines and the need to stay in bed automatically lessen the number of human contacts in the sick person's life. This may lead to disintegration and depression. Experiments with sensory deprivation have shown that people deprived of human contact quickly lose their psychological integrity. And depression in the dying patient may be due not to the anticipated loss but to the pain of separation.[15]

Yalom differentiates three kinds of social isolation: interpersonal, intrapersonal, and existential.[16] *Interpersonal* isolation is defined as a loneliness deriving from lack of intimacy and human contact. Robert was sixty-three years old. He had had lung cancer for nine years. His wife had died years ago, they had no children, and he was dying alone in the hospital. The day before he died, he asked to see a Kara counselor. He spoke mostly about everyday events. He was tough and uncomfortable about asking for help. "I'm wasting your time. All I need is a new pair of lungs." The counselor asked if he was afraid to die. He said, "No, not dying. I'm not afraid of that. But being alone is so scary. Lying here in the hospital late at night when it's dark and quiet and no one around is scary. I feel very alone then." The counselor told him to call her then if he wanted to. "Thank you, thank you for understanding." Then he returned the conversation to other things. The counselor noted genuine relief on his face. He died the next morning with the counselor holding his hand.

Intrapersonal loneliness occurs when a person feels isolated from a part of himself. Such loneliness can be experienced at any time in life, but it may be accentuated by the event of dying or grieving. For example, a widow who identified with her husband and is grieving his loss may also be grieving the loss of her own identity. She is no longer part of a couple and must readjust to the world as a single person. Intrapersonally she will feel isolated until she redefines herself as a solitary person.

Sylvia is a forty-four year old widow. Her husband died suddenly, and ten months later she still talks about him in the present tense. She has not yet cleared his clothes out of the closet. She feels that if she lets go of her grief, she will betray him. She does not want to talk about him to anyone: "If I share him I'll lose him." She wants her counselor to come visit her, but she does not want any contact with the counselor when she's there. She does not have close friends and will not acknowledge that she is grieving. She is quite confused and has taken few steps to re-enter life because she says she does not know who she is without her husband.

Existential isolation often underlies both interpersonal and intrapersonal isolation. It is the experience of being exposed to nothingness, our ultimate separateness. It is a fundamental source of the pain of human consciousness. Of existential isolation Erich Fromm wrote:

> ... the awareness of his aloneness and separateness, of his helplessness before the forces of nature and of society, all this makes his separate disunited existence an unbearable prison ... The experience of separateness arouses anxiety; it is indeed the source of all anxiety. Being separate means being cut off, without any capacity to use my human powers.[17]

But existential isolation need not be unbearably painful. The poet Rilke saw that it could be a source of joy and a means of deepening human relationships:

> ... once the realization is accepted that even between the *closest* human beings infinite distances continue to exist, a wonderful living side by side can grow up, if they succeed in loving the distance between them which makes it possible for each to see the other whole and against a wide sky.[18]

Frost was succinct and philosophical:

They cannot scare me with their empty spaces

Between stars—on stars where no human race is.
I have it in me so much nearer home
To scare myself with my own desert places.[19]

For the counselor: Many experts feel that during the chronic phase of dying, it is important to provide another focus for the client's life by encouraging him to engage in everyday tasks, and to develop and maintain supportive relationships. The counselor, however, must remain open to discussing the upcoming death and not try to divert all a patient's attention to other tasks.

During the terminal stage, the client needs to be given free reign with regard to who he wants to be with and how frequently he wants to see them. He needs to create a community of support so that he will not be alone if he does not want to be. His community cannot keep him from feeling his ultimate aloneness, but it can insure that he will not die totally isolated.

Fear of Loss of Family and Friends

The dying person is not only facing the loss of his own life. He is also grieving the loss of those he loves. It is important to allow him to go through this grieving process, since anticipatory grief is all he will have a chance to experience.

The dying person not only must anticipate the loss of the people he loves; he also experiences an altered relationship with them as his condition worsens. He becomes more dependent and others' responses to him may change as he experiences a loss of control and dignity. Basic patterns that have been established over many years may shift.

Many women Kara clients have been completely drained by caring for their dying husbands. Financial resources are depleted. The wife is emotionally and physically exhausted, and has little time to attend to her own needs. Undergoing anticipatory grief, she may feel a sense of separation from her husband and resulting guilt. If the husband was the strong, independent partner, turning the tables may influence every aspect of the relationship. He may be humiliated by the role reversal or he may enjoy being nurtured, but either way the relationship will have radically changed. Having a spouse who is dying does not automatically erase the caregiver's resentment, frustration, or anger at the fact of his dying. Latent problems in the relationship may arise as a result of the increased stress, and feelings of love and hate often emerge simultaneously. The negative feelings likely will be more laced with guilt than usual and must be considered with openness and acceptance by the counselor.

For the counselor: It is important to support family and friends by acknowledging the stress of the situation and the ever-changing flow of emotions. Clear communication should be aided and encouraged. The dying person needs reassurance about the strength and meaning of his relationships. He needs to say goodbye in his own way, as do the other members of the family.

Carol's mother had been dying for three years, and Carol had been the primary caregiver. She felt exhausted and drained for the entire time. She wished her mother would die and talked to her Kara counselor about how much she needed support for her feelings of frustration, anger, and guilt. Carol's own family was suffering from the strain of her frequent absences, but the children resented having to visit their dying grandmother when she brought them along.

Right before her mother died, the two of them had an important talk about Carol's difficulties and her mother's grief about losing her daughter and her family. The emotional conversation ended with some resolution for both. Carol was relieved when her mother died and grateful that she was at peace. It seemed a positive experience for both of them. She described the dying moment as creating a "connectedness between them and a lightness in the room." Her mother had a peaceful and calm expression on her face. The mutual acceptance in their connection before and at the time of her death overcame Carol's previous feelings of frustration and guilt. She felt it had healed her deeply.

Fear of Loss of Body and Identity

The body is an important element of our self-image. As the body image is distorted, questions of identity often arise. The loss of identity, of the self, may elicit feelings of embarrassment, inadequacy, and confusion. Loss of control compounds the problem. The usual ways that a person establishes identity are not available to the dying person, and a shift must occur in the attitudes of both the dying person and those around him.

The dying person may be disfigured from illness or the treatment he receives. He may begin to hate his body and want to hide from those around him. At Kara these reactions often occur at the onset of disfigurement, retreating into the background as death approaches. One Kara client, a woman who was once very beautiful, called us when she had become "very ugly." She had lost her hair through the course of treatment, had dark circles under her eyes, and was quite gaunt. She met her counselor in a wig and with carefully made-up face, an effect that undoubtedly took much effort to accomplish in her weakened condition. But in the last few months of her life, she stopped wearing the wig and make-up. She said that her priorities had changed, and how she looked had become secondary to her state of mind.

Limits to physical activity are often the first signs by which a person recognizes the reality of his or her own illness. For example, Rachel was diagnosed with a brain tumor a year and a half before she needed to curtail her activity. She decided to live her life as fully as possible, and being an active woman, she filled her days with beauty and meaning. She started looking at the reality of her cancer only when physical pain meant her busy life had to stop. It was then that she began to feel the anger, depression, and confusion and began her journey as a cancer patient.

Another aspect of loss of identity comes into play when the patient has an illness affecting the personality centers in the brain. A number of Kara clients are wives of husbands who have Alzheimer's disease, a degenerative condition that often affects middle-aged men. The body stays in relatively good condition, but the personality changes as the patient becomes senile and dependent. Suddenly, the wife finds herself taking care of her husband as if he were a child. When the disease is advanced, the patient needs twenty-four hour attention so he does not wander off. At this point, the wife often declares that her husband has become "another person" whom she does not know anymore. It is not clear what is happening with the patient at this point, but such degeneration may remind the counselor of the vulnerability of the personality.

Fear of loss of identity through death is often related to a person's spiritual viewpoint. If the physical being is the sum total of a person's identity, death will mean annihilation. If there is a belief in an identity beyond the physical body on earth, this loss will seem less final.

For the counselor: The primary task for the counselor is to help the client maintain a sense of dignity. This includes supporting his grieving over lost functions and appearance. It is important to recognize the dying person's uniqueness and to continue to relate to the parts of him that are still intact. Pattison reminds us to relate to the patient as a living person with a special story that makes up his life. If the dying person is given respect and appreciation as a living individual, he will be less likely to experience himself as lacking identity. Continued contact with what is familiar and habitual will help the dying person to realize that he is still who he always was.[20]

The counselor can give accurate feedback to the client about his body. He can help the client obtain realistic information about what is happening and what is likely to happen next. He should maintain an open attitude that assures the client that he is not a disgrace.

Fear of Regression

Regression is defined as the breakdown of the normal personality structure and defenses. It often occurs near death when the usual way of experiencing the self and the world changes.

Under any kind of stress a person may regress to earlier stages. The dying person needs touch and contact. He will make bargains and have fantasies about his death. He often will not believe death is coming until it is extremely obvious. He may express a strong desire for concrete information about his condition. Regression is normal and serves a person in understanding and integrating the stressful event. Fear of regression comes from a sense that this way of being will be permanent until death. This may or may not be true.

The dying process seems to initiate a gradual return to the dependence of infancy, which increases the possibility of regression. As death comes nearer, there is often a shift from active relating to the world of passive withdrawal.

The dying person seems instinctively to retreat from this world and enter a state of boundary-less non-being. This may be frightening to people who are uncomfortable with indefinite boundaries and unused to a lack of concrete activity. Dying and grieving people also struggle to resist the shift.

For the counselor: The most important thing the counselor can offer at this stage is sincere acceptance and support of the dying person's regression and his retreat from everyday reality to the withdrawn internal state. This can be described as the death of the psyche, and it is a major step in turning away from life and towards death.

Fear of Pain

When Kara counselors are asked in training what they fear the most about dying, many say that their worst fear is pain. One trainee observed that this was the first time she realized that before she dies she may experience pain that she cannot now even imagine, and this fact scared her more than death itself.

Usually a person tightens against the experience of pain, trying to control it by holding on. Anyone with chronic pain knows how useless this is, but if we ever give in to feeling our pain, physical or emotional, we need to surrender control. And that can be very frightening.

Pain and suffering often go together. But pain is only a sensation; it is our attitude towards it that interprets it as suffering. Pain is a perfect metaphor for the idea of surrendering to our lives, instead of resisting by needing to control.

Most of us fear pain, and our own fear influences how we reinforce the dying person's resistance to his pain. Intense pain often seems unmanageable, but it can be alleviated to some degree when the patient is supported in examining his pain and his attitude towards it. Attitudinal changes can deeply affect the way the dying person meets his death. The surrendering to pain may help him to find new meanings at the end of his life. Suffering has often been described as without meaning. But a person's attitude towards pain, as much as the treatment of it, can affect the amount of relief he feels.

For the counselor: To help the dying person minimize his suffering, it is useful to keep him from feeling isolated and to support him as he seeks ways to engage in life. It is also important to support him in choosing the kind of pain management he wants to undertake. If he feels that he has made his own choices, he will be less likely to suffer.

The counselor's own relationship with pain deeply affects his work with clients. The most difficult task is "hanging out" with another's pain without trying to fix it, change it, or stop it. This act requires the counselor to experience his own helplessness and anguish without running away or acting out, to face his own pain with open eyes.

Some pain cannot be taken away, but it may be able to be worked through. This is true for emotional as well as physical pain. When a client is in severe emotional pain, miracles can occur if he has a counselor or friend who is willing to maintain contact to the bottom of the pain. This is one of the greatest gifts a person can give. It is a matter of paying close attention and feeling whatever comes up as both client and counselor experience the pains of loss and dying.

When it comes to physical pain, there is much that caregivers can do. Besides traditional and non-traditional medical care, alternative attitude techniques can be taught. These include hypnosis, meditation, the Simonton visualization technique,[21] and the Center for Attitudinal Healing's visualization work.[22] Much of this work with physical pain affects emotional pain as well and has proven very effective.

Denial

In grieving or in coming to terms with death, the phase of denial seems especially important because it so easily can be used in a self-destructive way. Denial is the state of avoiding or blocking the experience of what may otherwise be or seem obvious. Situational denial may occur when one is looking at one's own impending death or at the death of another. This type of defense occurs in response to a shock in one's life.

It is important to note that denial serves an essential purpose in life. It is not always dysfunctional, but can be a healthy means of integrating shocking material into our consciousness by a process involving incremental learning. A person can bite off small bits of knowledge at a time, digest them, and use them to redefine his world view, only then returning to seek more information.

A counselor, frustrated by the lack of action in a case, may comment that a client is "stuck in denial." This counselor needs to develop respect for, and humility about, the ways we protect ourselves as we cope with the pain of loss. One thing is certain: the way a person normally relates to life is apt to be radically different from the way he would relate to it if he were in pain.

On the other hand, denial, like all forms of defense, can be used inappropriately. It is not the counselor's role to decide when a client is "stuck"—that is for the client to decide. Caregivers should only reflect their own responses to the client's feelings and actions.

Yalom cites a patient who, at age twenty-eight, was told by her surgeon that she had cervical cancer and that she would live only about six more months.[23] The surgeon also told this to her parents. Only an hour later her radiotherapist told her they were going to try to cure her. She chose to believe him. She spent the next few months at her parents' home being treated as if she were going to die while she thought she was recovering. Her parents insulated her from the world and hovered around her. Finally the misunderstanding was cleared up. Her parents realized that she might live and stopped the "royal" treatment, but the woman was deeply upset by the experience:

> Because of the error and a miscommunication I was already dead to my family, and I started being dead and it was a very hard way back to get myself to be alive. It was worse later on as I was getting better than it was when I was very sick because when the family suddenly realized that I was getting better then they left and went back to their daily chores and I was still left with being dead and I couldn't handle it very well. I'm still frightened and trying to cross the boundary line that seems to be in front of me—the boundary line of, am I dead or am I alive?[24]

We should be wary about making generalizations about denial or other defenses. There is a difference between the *process* of denial and the *fact* of denial. The process of denial is fluid and may be full or partial at any given moment. It is not a constant, but a changing perception of given facts. Denial is an opportunity for reality testing, both for the caregiver and for the patient.[25]

Denial is situational. It is not only an avoidance response in the face of danger, but also an act to prevent loss of a significant relationship. Therefore patients may deny more to one person than to another. Denial helps to maintain a constant relationship with others, especially when there is a crisis.[26]

For the counselor: While a counselor should not make the superficial judgment that a client is "stuck in denial," it is also important that he not support the denial beyond what is appropriate. He should support facing the feelings beneath the denial, while at the same time respecting the client's own timing and needs. The client will be able to tell the difference between a counselor who is invested in his denial and one who is open to looking at it.

Depression

When working with a client who has cancer or some other long-term illness, the counselor will note that anxiety tends to be the dominant experience before treatment begins. After the period of anxiety is over, depression often sets in.

Depression and anger represent two possible emotional responses to the fear and helplessness of illness and impending death. They are related: behind anger one often finds tears of despair, and behind deep sadness are often waves of rage.

Patients with long-term illness are facing a gamut of new stresses and experiences. They feel out of control of both their illness and their treatment. They become suddenly dependent on their family and fear of becoming a burden may lead them to isolate themselves from others. Family members also may become depressed about their own lack of control and fearful as they consider their own futures. Dealing with the patient's emotions as well as their own and feeling responsible for care may bring on depression in members of a patient's family.

There are two basic types of depression: agitated and retarded.[27] Agitated depression is accompanied by an underlying feeling of hopelessness, worthlessness, and isolation. It is expressed as agitated activity and restlessness. Retarded depression involves the same feelings, but people affected in this way are paralyzed by the situation. They are overwhelmed by their situation and cannot move.

These two states may co-exist. A Kara client of many years found that he had cancer and that the prognosis was poor. He gave away all his possessions and moved to a cabin in the woods, far from all his friends. For weeks he stayed in bed and even went hungry. Unable to motivate himself to cook, he would not ask his friends for help. Eventually, his friends convinced him to move back with them in town. Slowly he found he could accept more help. His depression shifted at this point, and he became agitated. He displayed a deep restlessness and dissatisfaction with everything and everyone. He moved out of his friends' house into a small apartment and shortly thereafter asked his Kara counselor to move in to clean and cook for him. At the same time, he often missed appointments with the counselor and was unable to focus on anything when they did meet. He began a relationship with a woman who eventually moved into his home. It was then that he started to talk about "really living" until he died.

Depression can also come from an emotional response to illness or from an internal physical imbalance. This can occur as a result of medical treatment or exhaustion from stress.

There is a less common type of depression called preparatory depression, which occurs in a dying patient who is mourning the loss of his life, relationships, and strength.[28] Preparatory depression may present itself in bizarre dreams, fantasies, unexplainable sadness, anorexia, or apathy. Suicide may be considered from an objective position.

For the counselor: For the client who is in agitated or retarded depression, it is helpful to focus on the concrete and mobilize him to the best of his abilities. For example, the counselor might help him schedule physical activity that he enjoys and teach him ways to avoid hurting himself emotionally, along with ways to promote self-nurturance. The counselor can make the client aware that he perceives him as a strong person, capable of living up to his own expectations.

The counselor may want to help the client find practical solutions to solvable problems such as those involving finances and communications. In the process, the counselor may help the client define exactly what is causing his depression.

The best way to behave with a client in preparatory depression is just to be there. There are no solutions; the grief is real, and there is no way out. The client is experiencing closure on his life and needs respect and support.

Anger

Our culture seems to have the same taboos about expressing anger as the Victorians had about sexuality. It is often easier for a person to move into depression than anger. This is especially true when the anger is at God, at a trusted doctor, or at the person who died, or perhaps at a terminally ill husband who is making life so difficult. It is hard to express anger without feeling guilty. There seems a lot to lose by expressing anger while facing death, but anger is one of the most appropriate responses to this shock.

The high cost of not expressing anger is illustrated by a former Kara client who was in her twenties when she was diagnosed as having Hodgkins disease. She called Kara because she knew she was dying and needed to talk about it. When the counselor saw her, she spoke of her fear of being alone and of her rage at her illness and at everyone who was healthy. She was most terrified of asking for help and was determined to die independently. Soon after her initial contact with Kara, her condition worsened dramatically. Hospitalized, she refused to see her friends, her family, or her counselor. She died alone in the hospital, angry and rejecting.

Anger is especially avoided because of the fear that others will reject us when we most need them. This client's fear was so deep-rooted that it was easier for her to reject first than to face possible rejection by those around her. Dying people need to feel permission to express anger without fear of repercussions from doctors, family, or friends. (This is true for all of us, of course, throughout our lives.)

> The inability to experience one's anger leads to diminished physical resistance and symptoms of depression. But the ability to tolerate the experience of anger is a step towards wholeness. One is able to make contact with feelings, with possible modes of expression, with alternative choices, and with a sense of personal authority.[29]

Acceptance of the anger of a dying person further affirms the acceptance of his being and helps him to be an active participant rather than a helpless victim. The choice to express anger can be a turning point for the patient in recognizing that he is the creator of his own emotional reaction to his death.

For the counselor: With an angry client the counselor should listen actively without taking the anger personally. Anger can help the client improve the quality of his life. The counselor can help to focus anger into appropriate channels through careful listening and responding and to bring out other feelings along with the anger—like fear, isolation, vulnerability, hopelessness, or lack of control. It is important to match the intensity of the client's words; using less intense words may give the impression that the full strength of the anger is not acceptable, while more intense words may make the client feel that he is not understood.

Hope

In the first moments of learning about an impending death, hope comes in the form of an expectation of remission, cure, or many years of healthy life. Hope is an important element in getting well or living fully.

As much as our attitude affects our health, hope will influence the course of an illness.

Stotland differentiates between the "expectational" hope for a cure and the hope of the dying person who has recognized the terminal nature of the disease. He calls the latter "desirable hope" and defines it as changing the expectation of survival to a recognition that it is desirable but not likely to happen.[30] Since with this recognition the patient may psychologically give up fighting for life, it is ideal that expectational hope not end until right before the patient begins to withdraw from his environment.

It is important to watch the dynamics of hope in a dying patient and his family. It can be used as a defensive avoidance of the reality of the situation. But there is a fine line between realistic and unrealistic hope; the decision about whether the hope is realistic or not is purely subjective. The counselor must put aside his own prejudices and try to determine whether the patient's and family's expression of hope is appropriate to the situation.

For the counselor: It is important to remember that hope can influence survival. Victor Frankl, describing his experiences in Nazi concentration camps, observes that those who survived lived on hope alone, hope for nothing but life itself.[31] The nature of hope changes continually during the course of the illness. It is useful to support the client in relinquishing and grieving the loss of old goals and in modifying his vision of new attainable goals.

> Modification of goals is seen in those chronically ill and terminal patients who are able to remain hopeful. Hope and denial go hand in hand, but denial is intermittent. Each new treatment restores hope; each setback brings back the reality of the final end. Reports from terminal patients indicate that the ability to relinquish expectations is a factor in maintaining hope.[32]

Positive and Negative Thoughts and Emotions

It is generally accepted that there may be some connection between our emotions and thoughts and the outcome of a given situation. Simonton has had much success with positive imagery influencing the course of the illness in cancer patients.[33] LeShan concluded, after many studies of cancer patients, that hope does influence the patient's lifespan.[34] Others have found that the lack of a loving relationship may precipitate illness.[35] On the other hand, "positive thinking" can sometimes be an avoidance of what is happening internally. If grief, fear, or anger is a dominant emotion of the dying patient, positive thinking will be only a smokescreen and any positive imagery biased by these underlying emotions.

A fifty-six year old woman came to Kara with her husband. Speaking for both of them, the husband said that his wife had cancer and asked for a counselor. He then proceeded to talk about how she would recover and everything would be fine. Like a cheerleader frantically supporting a losing team, he insisted it was time to marshal their resources. Later, when the woman saw a counselor alone, a dam burst, and she tearfully expressed all the fears, anger, and pain that she could not express at home. In her case, her husband's insistence on positive thinking only emphasized the discrepancy with her real feelings and compounded her grief and alienation from him.

The feelings expressed by a woman who was separating from her husband bring to light some of the difficulties in thinking "too positively." This woman said that she was afraid to mourn the relationship and feel the pain of the separation because, with the expression of grief would come full knowledge that the relationship was over. Thinking positively might influence the outcome and lead towards a reconciliation. She was afraid she would indulge in her grief, and that negativity would obliterate the hope that was there. But something is missing from this argument. Our task is to acknowledge all that is happening emotionally as nonjudgmentally as possible. A person may need to hold hope and positive thinking in one hand and pain and grief in the other. The counselor may need to remind a client that emotions do not arise in an orderly non-contradictory manner, and negative thoughts do not, in themselves, create negative situations. An onslaught of negative emotion can be compared to a thunderstorm: it rushes in, drenches the land, and then pulls back. Negative emotions are made negative only by our ideas about them, past experiences of them, and our fear of them. The experience of pure emotion is neither positive nor negative and is generally a release, an opportunity to feel deeply inside ourselves.

It is an extraordinary feat to try to accept the inevitable without becoming passive, to admit that fate is out of our hands yet not surrender completely. All we can do is experience the emotions that arise. In this way we will be doing everything we can to help ourselves. This requires an internal strength and peace of mind, which can be developed through practice with the losses and hopes in everyday life.

Acceptance

The term acceptance has been much abused in the area of death and dying. It is common for people to consider denial as unacceptable and acceptance as the ideal state for a dying person to attain. Acceptance and denial are multifaceted experiences that cannot be simply defined. As with hope and despair, denial and acceptance often accompany each other in the experience of dying. A dying person often will accept some parts of his situation while rejecting others.

Acceptance can be defined as allowing the event to occur without resistance. The act of acceptance can take many forms. It may be a dramatic act of surrendering after a long battle or it may be a simple decision. It may be an acceptance of the reality of death, of love from a caregiver, or of the loss of a spouse or the function of a limb.

Acceptance may develop in a variety of ways. Nancy, aged sixty-five, had lung cancer but continued to smoke non-stop in her nursing home bed. During the early days of her stay at the home, she was angry at having to eat meatloaf and carrots five times a week, angry at nurses who took her cigarettes away, and angry at aides who ignored her calls. She wanted to go home to her waterbed. Eventually though, with the consistent attention of her counselor and friends, she came closer to recognizing her impending death. She spent her last weeks buying stuffed animals for the other nursing home patients, "so they can have something to stroke and love." She felt accepted and loved by the nurses and wanted to return their love. Her attitude of resistance had radically changed to one of acceptance of all those around her. The last day of her life, she envisioned her death as a "flying away." The attention and connection she was given in her last days probably contributed to her peaceful attitude in the end.

Unlike Nancy, Rebecca did not get outwardly angry, but chose to keep her life as active as possible. Still alive at this writing, Rebecca is in her fifties. She has cancer of the colon, liver, and lung. When she heard her diagnosis, she fully believed it and began practical plans with her husband about where and how he would live after her death. Opting for quality rather than quantity of life, she chose not to have chemotherapy or any other treatment, and at first she felt no ill effects. She and her husband continued their traveling and hiking. She did not talk much about her illness; she wanted to enjoy what life was left as fully as possible. Her fears were not of death but of being physically inactive, of becoming dependent, weak, and in pain.

Lately, Rebecca has been in more pain and is talking more about her illness, but she is not despairing. She is up and about in her garden. Aware that she will die, she is choosing every day how she wants to live and appreciating the precious normality of her life at this moment.

In sharp contrast was Donna, who found she had cancer of the liver at the age of sixty-five. Donna refused to accept the fact of her death up until her last week. She talked about how she would get better and about the new treatments she would try. She was planning what to wear to her daughter's upcoming wedding, even though she couldn't walk. She never said, "I'm scared," or "I'm dying," but she seemed to come to a point where her body said it for her. She was not eating much and was getting progressively sicker. She didn't talk, but others sensed that she thought it was the end. There was a feeling of peace and acceptance in her room the week before she died. She became withdrawn, did not talk or reach out to anyone, yet the last day her counselor saw her she squeezed the counselor's hand and thanked her.

Another case provides a classic example of working through grief to acceptance and growth. Connie, age fifty-eight, is grieving the loss of her husband. When he died she had no supportive family relationships and spent much time feeling lonely and isolated. She was unsure of herself and fearful that she could not survive alone, and she experienced a long period of depression during which she questioned her purpose in life. After this, she made several attempts to rejoin the world, but found her sense of personal inadequacy kept her from being successful. Then, eleven months after his death, she began to emerge from her depression and to believe in herself more. She joined a widows group and considered working. She now feels pain and grief, but has slowly and gently begun to live her life again. Unable to sleep for months, she recently realized that her husband's picture by the bed was the last thing she looked at every night. She has moved it—as well as other things he left behind. She feels a tremendous growth and satisfaction with herself and the course of her griefwork.

Finally, the following case study explores the role of acceptance in a family situation. Dan and Beth were a special couple, and their example can teach us many lessons about saying goodbye. They had decided to have a baby when Dan was diagnosed as having terminal brain cancer. Against the doctor's recommendations, they conceived their child that same week. Dan had tremendous strength and beat all odds to live past his baby's first birthday, but the tumor did prevail.

One evening, when Dan recognized that he was dying, he called all his friends over and said goodbye to each of them personally. Though he lived two weeks more, this evening was the last truly lucid one he had. On the morning of his death, Beth called the Kara counselor, Mary, to their house. She wanted Mary's support in making the decisions she anticipated she would have to make. When Mary got there, she and Beth knelt by Dan's bed. He was in a coma with his eyes almost closed. Beth had been talking to him, asking him to squeeze her finger in response. This squeezing had gotten progressively weaker. Mary asked Beth if Dan knew what was happening to him. Beth did not know. She whispered, close to his ear, "Dan, you're in a coma and having a lot of trouble breathing." He immediately stopped struggling to breathe. Through her tears, she told him who was in the room and where their baby was. Her voice was comforting and seemed to help him feel peaceful. She told him, "Maybe God is calling you today. I want you to know, as much as I love you, if it's time for you to go, it's OK with me. I can go on. I'll miss you very, very much, but I'll manage."

The nurse came on duty, and Beth left to take a shower. Mary went into the other room and opened her book, *The Course in Miracles*, to this passage: "All we have to realize is that we are not our bodies, and we can communicate without them if we want."[36] She returned to Dan's bed and sat about a foot away. The nurse had his hand in hers and was rubbing it gently. Mary thought, "Dan, you are beautiful, and it's really all right for you to die now." During the next few moments several events occurred simultaneously. Beth was coming down the stairs as the phone rang. Dan's parents answered the phone in the kitchen near the bedroom. The nurse got up and left the room to respond to the call. As she let go of his hand and walked out, he exhaled his last breath. He simply did not breathe in again. Mary felt a surge of gentle energy through her body from her feet to her head and felt it rising up to the ceiling, getting bigger. Time stood still for her. She had no thoughts, only the sensation of energy. This moment was broken by Dan's mother running to the doorway, "Did he stop breathing?" Dan's parents, and Beth, returned to the bedroom crying and touching his face. Beth told him how much she loved him, and the group spent the next hour sitting on the bed with his body, weeping, praying, and talking. Finally they called the coroner and began to phone relatives.

Early in the morning after her husband died, Beth climbed to the top of the local football stadium and screamed as loud as she could: "Dan, how could you leave me?" "How could you do this to me?" She described this later by saying she "let it rip." In the months to come she continued to give expression to her grief. While accepting the fact of his death, she also raged into the night until exhaustion. She experienced sadness, laughter, peace, fear, and anger in continuous cycles.

Beth and Dan demonstrated, throughout his illness, and in her subsequent grief, how acceptance, denial, rage, and sadness can appear concurrently. Their process is a fine example of the act of acceptance. They were willing to see what was happening in the moment and experience it as fully as possible without cutting themselves off.

For the counselor: As can be seen in all of these cases, working with the dying and grieving can be a very moving experience, no matter what emotions are being expressed. Pattison described the counselor role well when he said:

First, there are varying degrees of denial and acceptance of death within each individual that vary over the living-dying interval. Second, there are always contradictions between the conscious-rational and the unconscious-emotional aspects of both denial and acceptance. Third, our task as helpers is not to eliminate denial and attain absolute acceptance with the dying. Rather, we face the more human task of responding to a flowing process of both denial and acceptance in ourselves and the dying.[37]

THE TERMINAL PHASE

This phase begins roughly when the dying person begins to withdraw from his environment and spends a great deal of time focusing inward. This withdrawal can also be described as a "giving up" or deepening of depression.[38] The change from expectational hope to desirable hope (see earlier section on hope) often stimulates withdrawal. However, in some cases withdrawal stimulates the change.

One characteristic of this withdrawal is a shift in the dying person's concept of time and space. It may be helpful to consider the perceptions of the dying as similar to those of a newborn. The focus may be almost totally inward and with little awareness of or interest in the daily events of life. Yet there still is an adult human being, with all his years of life, experiencing these moments. An example follows.

An artist and poet in her youth, Denny is now one hundred seven years old. At age one hundred three, she needed nursing care. Now she has a cataract in her left eye, can barely see in her right eye, hardly moves, does not talk, and never gets out of bed. She is emaciated, but seems instinctively to eat anything put near her mouth. She had hearing aids that allowed her to hear a little, but now no one puts them on her; they don't seem to make much difference. Denny is not sick. She is very, very old. What is her world like now? Is she like an infant? How can she stand to live in this dark, silent world of hers? Recently she curled into the fetal position and cannot be moved out of it. But she eats every day. Some part of her, instinctive or conscious, does not want to die.

During the terminal stage there is a different consciousness of time. Chronological time is one of the structures we create to make sense of our lives and to aid communication and connection. Most people have probably had moments in their lives when they were sick, happy, overwhelmed, or in some other emotional state and time became irrelevant. According to Weisman, there are two ways that time can be defined. Chronological time, he says, quantifies events according to physical space and location. Existential time qualifies events according to their personal significance.[39]

Chronological time follows the linear model of experiencing the world. Existential time is more like the Buddhist definition, in which past, present, and future appear as different angles of viewing the same moment. Existential time is personal and reflects the inner nature of the individual. Unlike chronological time, it has no measurements except experience itself. It is reflected in the rhythms of the body and is oriented to internal processes. In the midst of existential time there is no past or future—only the present. A particularly dramatic but not uncommon example of existential time occurs when a person in a near-death accident perceives time and space as stretching out. Each moment becomes its own eternity.

Time for a dying person often is only existential. The quality of the person's life experience is of more importance than the quantity of events. The dying person will not have the same perceptions and priorities as the person not anticipating imminent death. The process of dying occurs in existential time and has little to do with what is observed by others. This is why it is so important for the counselor to discard his preconceptions about the way interactions with a dying person should go.

Different Types of Death

Dying involves different kinds of deaths, all of which may occur simultaneously but often come at different times. There is controversy over precisely when life ends. Physically, it ends with brain death and cessation of the heartbeat. Socially, death may come sooner if the patient has been ostracized by family, friends, or doctors. Psychologically, dying begins when the patient withdraws and no longer makes contact with the environment.[40] Kalish asked students to determine when they thought death actually occurs. His results are shown below.[41]

Condition	% of Students
When the heart stops beating	52%
When the person loses self-awareness	35%
When the person wishes to die or gives up	35%
Entering the hospital or nursing home, knowing he will never leave again	14%
Learning of a terminal diagnosis	4%
Becoming senile	4%
People never die or don't die at time of physical death	18%

Physical death. As each organ dies, the patient suffers a biological death. But he may not actually die. For full biological death to occur, he must cease functioning as an organism.

> So some parts of me may far outlast "that which is me" and some parts of me will die before "that which is me" dies. We don't disagree much about those parts; what we disagree about is when the "one" dies. For this to happen, the organism that is "me" must cease to function as an organism and, given our present state of knowledge, the cessation must be irreversible. When this event occurs, the legal definition of death has been met, and the death certificate can be signed.[42]

Social death. Social death can occur long before physical death. It can happen as the patient is moved to a nursing home, or when he is diagnosed as terminal and largely ignored in a hospital room, or as the family withdraws and leaves the patient alone to die. It occurs when the dying person is no longer recognized by his family or friends as living.

Being discounted as socially dead can lead quickly to loss of hope and meaning. When the dying person's need for support is not met, his will to live diminishes. Kalish cites this example:

> Jonas was an elderly man who had lived in the nursing home for four years, ever since his 81st birthday, when his children decided that they could no longer care for him in their home without disrupting their own families. However, all three of his children, numerous grandchildren, and his aging wife, who was crippled with severe arthritis and living with a somewhat spry sister, came to visit often. Jonas received at least two visits every week, and often more.

> Then, within a brief period of time, his wife died, his oldest son became seriously ill with cancer, and his daughter's husband retired and she moved with him to Florida. Although he was somewhat confused, Jonas was alert enough to know what was happening, and his deep concern for his son plus his feeling of being abandoned by his wife and daughter led to a kind of stress that he had great difficulty handling. As visits dropped off and his depression deepened, he became increasingly confused. Then, as the licensed vocational nurse tending his unit said, "When I had to tell him his son had died, I could see the change. He just turned his face to the wall and didn't say a thing. And he hardly ate after that. One morning when I went to give him breakfast, I saw his face covered with tears. He was unconscious when I returned for the tray and

had died by that afternoon."[43]

Psychological death. This kind of death comes as the patient withdraws from his environment. Social death and death of the psyche are closely connected. Feeling disoriented and unrecognized can lead to withdrawal, and the patient's withdrawal can influence others not to pay attention to him. This can lead to further deterioration.

Physiological death. A person is physiologically dead when he goes into a deep coma or loses brain function, becoming totally unaware of both himself and his environment. At this point he is unaware not only of *who* he is but also *that* he is.[44]

Pattison constructed a table describing the variety of ways a patient can die, which appears as Figure 2. He describes biological death as the death of organs, physiological death as the cessation of awareness, psychological death as the state of withdrawal, and sociological death as the withdrawal of others. He identifies the possible consequences of the social rejection of the patient, the denial of the fact of the impending death, the patient's rejection of life, the prolongation of the patient's life through artificial means, and his perception of the ideal death. Pattison feels that ideally all four types of death should occur as closely as possible to each other, but not necessarily simultaneously.

FIGURE 2.
POSSIBLE DISTORTIONS TO THE PROCESS OF DYING*

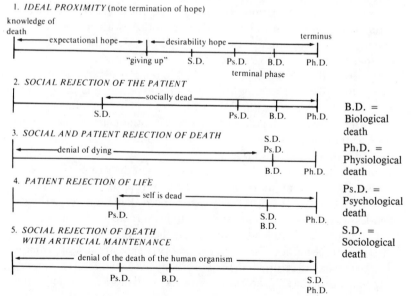

*Source: E.M. Pattison, *The Experience of Dying,* Englewood Cliffs, N.J.: Prentice-Hall, 1977, p. 57.

For the counselor: What is a "good" death? Many of us have an image of the ideal way to die and may be tempted to impose that ideal on the client. Weisman shifts the focus from that of a good death to that of an *appropriate* death.[45] The counselor, family, and friends cannot impose dignity, integrity, or honor on the dying person. They can only provide the opportunity or the environment for him to die in the best way he knows how. The appropriate and "best" death is one in which the person ends his life in the way he chooses.

III. POST-LOSS GRIEF: MOURNING

"I'll be out running and I'll say, 'I could run from here to San Francisco airport if it would bring my Dad back.' Or I could swim from now until three hours from now without stopping if that would bring him back. Or, I could do ten massages in a row with no breaks. You know I just have all these bargains going and I'm fooling myself. I know I'm fooling myself. I keep thinking what wouldn't I do. Is there anything I wouldn't do? I haven't found anything. I would do anything, just anything."

—Kara client in Kara
slide presentation, 1980.

Recently, at Kara, three mothers with newborn infants were talking. They were amazed at how each baby had the same shudders run through him, how each one sounded like the others with his mewing cry, and how they all had similar hand and leg motions. Yet, each child was obviously unique, with his or her own personality and style.

Patterns of similarity also can be seen in the process of grieving and dying, but at the same time each person's experience is unique and special. In fact, the most important thing to understand about grief is that while there are some general tendencies, there are no rules. The counselor or other caregiver must be prepared to support each person's own style and process of grieving.

Only through grieving freely can the depths of the wound of a loss be healed. Many clients have asked if they were crazy because of the emotions and loss of control they experienced. Each felt very relieved and less isolated when told that his feelings were normal.

Many grieving people also worry that their pain is lasting too long. "It's been three months," they may say. "My friends are sick of my pain. The family has all returned to their everyday lives, and I hurt as if it just happened yesterday!" Grieving often takes much more time than people are willing to allow. The Jewish ritual of waiting a year to uncover the headstone is more realistic. In fact, the grieving process can take more than a year. In some ways, it never ends, but only changes.

Three phases of post-loss grief are commonly recognized: a phase of numbing disbelief, an acute grief phase, and a reorganization or resolution phase.[46] The phase of numbing shock and disbelief may last an hour or a week. It is followed by an acute state of grieving, which can last for months or years. The acute phase includes: a lessening of denial, pangs of distress, inconsistent or contradictory behavior, feelings of yearning, "searching" behaviors such as talking to the lost person, a sense that something is about to happen, aimlessness and restlessness, and a feeling that time has stopped. The person experiencing acute grief may be afraid of "going crazy," may regress to earlier modes of behavior, and may begin to take on characteristics of the deceased.

In the third and final phase of grieving reorganization and resolution take place. If the outcome is favorable it will include acceptance of the loss, memories that are less painful, a re-establishment of self-esteem, and a return to life with a new focus on the present and future. If the outcome is not favorable it will include acceptance of loss but with chronic depression, physical and emotional pains, and vulnerability to other losses.

The three phases of grief do not proceed in order. There is overlapping, and there is movement toward and movement away from resolution. Yet the general progression is from phase one to three. Let's look at each phase in more detail.

PHASE 1: NUMBING, SHOCK, DENIAL

This phase is a brief one reflecting an initial shocked response to the news. A person's sense of time changes, and everything seems blurred and unreal. In a numb and isolated cocoon, the grieving individual moves mechanically through required actions.

Sometimes people in shock appear stoical and unemotional. The numbness has kept them from feeling the impact of the loss. Even after the initial shock begins to wear away, the griever may vascillate between pain and numbness. "Because death is usually a fact we do not want to believe, it is a long, slow process to overcome our resistance and accept reality. The truth is that we keep hoping that we will awaken from this nightmare."[47]

The grieving person can be initially in a state of high physiological arousal, which may feel like panic. This panic or alarm can have a protective function, keeping a tidal wave of emotions at bay and allowing the reality of the event to be experienced incrementally. These episodes of panic often continue beyond the initial phase of shock.

Insomnia often occurs during this initial response, as well as an immediate ambivalence. The bereaved is torn between the past experience of the loved one being alive and the current news that he is gone. This ambivalence lasts well into the acute phase and even into reorganization. It includes the desire to be alone and the need to make contact with others. The bereaved alternates between past and future, despair and hope, wanting to forget and needing to remember, wanting to move ahead but needing to keep mementos. The warring parts are the urge to hold on to what has been lost and the desire to give it up and move on.

For the counselor: The counselor must allow the client to experience an intense and sometimes overwhelming surge of contradictory emotions. He needs to be willing to accept the client's pain with empathy and grace. He needs to control his own panic in the face of his client's and to understand the helplessness, aimlessness, rage, and sorrow. There is absolutely no problem to be solved here. The most the counselor can do is to provide an understanding, respectful presence, recognizing that the client's grief could well be his own.

Kalish describes his reactions to the news of the death of a friend:

> My first reaction after hanging up [after having heard of Don's death] and after a few moments of being with myself, was to send Don's wife a note. Somehow I could not do it—an overwhelming feeling kept pressing me to acknowledge, that, perhaps, a mistake had been made, and that such a note would only bring embarrassment or confusion. It took me a week to write this note. My next feeling was that I should send Don a note, telling him how sorry I was about . . . I wasn't sure about what. My selves watched each other struggle with this impossible thought, with only a thrust of reality that kept me from composing "Dear Don, I am sorry to hear that . . . but you will, of course, be . . . if there is anything . . . please . . ." This feeling remained for several days.
>
> Then the arithmetic. If Don is 55 and I am . . . then my youngest child will be . . . when I am 55, which means . . . while my oldest will be . . . or about ready to . . . and the middle . . .
>
> And finally the attempts to pull back from the view of my own termination. What had Don done to deserve to die? What was he doing that I was not doing, so his death did not mean I was also mortal? Did he elicit the wrath of God? Did he violate the laws of good health? Perhaps he neglected an annual physical or consumed too much butter or bourbon or bacon or . . .[48]

Kalish experienced sorrow, the urge to help, and his own personal understanding of how it could have been he who died. In depicting the shock of the bereaved he describes the emotions a counselor may feel as well.

PHASE 2: THE ACUTE GRIEF PHASE

Emerging awareness and intense emotion come when the reality of the loss hits home. The numbing subsides. Rage, anguish, weeping, and despair are not unusual emotions. Loneliness and childlike feelings of dependency and fear of abandonment may reappear. Guilt, fear, hostility, love, and ambivalence are often dominant emotions.

The pain tends to come and go in waves. Memories of the person keep flooding in. The mind feels very active, yet at the same time there is a sense of being overwhelmed and in a daze. Everyday memory and awareness may be vague and disoriented, with an ongoing sense of anxiety and jumpiness. C.S. Lewis writes: "No one told me grief is so much like fear. I am not afraid, but the sensation is like being afraid. The same fluttering in the stomach, the same restlessness, the yawning. I keep on swallowing."[49]

Grief generally is experienced not as prolonged depression, but as acute and episodic "pangs." The acute phase also is characterized by episodes of intense yearning, weeping, and distress, by insomnia, restlessness, and moments of panic. There is a preoccupation with thoughts of the person who died and events leading up to the death. This is stimulated by a feeling that something is about to happen. The bereaved may have dreams or hallucinations of the lost person and say that he has returned or is really alive. There may also arise some superstitious proofs that the death did not really occur. This searching behavior, with the urge to recover the deceased, is universal.[50]

Anger is another common feature of the acute phase of grieving. It is often episodic, alternating with depression or despair. Sometimes anger will be expressed as impatience or irritability. It probably will feel irrational to the bereaved and may induce guilt.

There are many factors that inhibit anger. These include the general cultural taboo and a personal style that avoids such emotions. But resistance to the outward expression of anger may create problems for the grieving person, since unexpressed anger may produce depression, self-hatred, guilt, or other self-destructive emotions. Clearly, a friend or counselor who can provide a safe environment for the expression of anger is very helpful. The counselor, however, should be aware that some people may use anger to cover up deeper emotions of sadness and betrayal.

Another characteristic of the acute phase of grieving is the attempt to take action to alleviate some of the pain. An example of this is a widow sleeping with pillows on her husband's side of the bed or talking to him. Many widows talk to their dead husbands, the degree of communication ranging from saying goodnight to his picture to carrying on conversations all day. Another common experience is feeling the presence of the dead person.

Counselors encountering this sense of presence in grieving clients may have some difficulty in interpreting the experience to the client. It could be a psychotic hallucination, a normal grief reaction, or an actual vision of the deceased. This issue is discussed often at Kara, and there is no pat answer to the problem. A trained counselor should be able to recognize a psychotic episode, and in the absence of such a disorder to simply reflect and support the phenomenological experience of the client.

The phenomenon of identification also occurs often during this phase. Taking on the characteristics of the dead person is one final attempt to insure that the loved one is not lost by making his traits a part of oneself. Identification can come in many forms. It can be an internal process that is not always behaviorally observable. When it is apparent externally, the bereaved may try on various characteristics of the deceased, reject them, and try on others. This is a healthy part of normal grief, though in less healthy forms identification may include taking on aspects of the dead spouse's last illness.

For the counselor: Griefwork needs to be done in solitude as well as with understanding companions. The counselor should allow the client to be vague and slow. recognizing that repetition is essential for internalization and eventual acceptance of the death.

The counselor needs to be able to tolerate denial, yet encourage the expression of emotions. The most important role the counselor can play is to create a safe place for the bereaved to express emotions. The counselor should not put a time limit on grief, reminding the client that when friends go back to their busy lives, the grief may still be raw. It is important to offer support for as long as it is needed and to provide a reality check for the client who wants to know what normal grief entails.

Perhaps the most important role the counselor can play during the acute phase of grieving is simply to provide the client with one person who is not afraid to talk about the experience of death and the pain and sadness that follow it. Many friends are self-conscious and unsure about how to approach a bereaved person, as C.S. Lewis observed after the death of his wife:

An odd byproduct of my loss is that I'm aware of being an

embarrassment to everyone I meet. At work, at the club, in the street, I see people, as they approach me, trying to make up their minds whether they'll "say something about it" or not. I hate it if they do, and if they don't. Some funk it altogether. R. has been avoiding me for a week. I like best the well brought-up young men, almost boys, who walk up to me as if I were a dentist, turn very red, get it over, and then edge away to the bar as quickly as they decently can. Perhaps the bereaved ought to be isolated in special settlements like lepers.[51]

PHASE 3: REORGANIZATION AND RESOLUTION

This phase implies a final ending to grief, which may be inaccurate. The acute grief reactions may become more infrequent, but missing someone may never end. Signs of reorganization do not mean an end to sadness. They indicate a willingness to continue with one's life and to take up new activities and meet new people.

The act of reorganization involves discarding old habits and identities and substituting new ones. Grief itself serves as the sculptor of the new identity. The shaping begins with the first thought of a hopeful future, the first inclination that new meaning is possible. Hidden in grief during the chaotic period, the new identity can be more clearly recognized when the bereaved starts to look up and take steps towards any goal. The cycles of belief and disbelief begin to slow down, and clear acknowledgment of the death emerges. Identification with the deceased is slowly relinquished, and a new separate identity begins to develop. Thought patterns shift from the past to the present and future.

Facing these changes may lead to a feeling of betrayal and many retreats into the past with the pain that is more familiar than the new aloneness that is emerging. It takes time to recognize that this new identity does not mean that the deceased is forgotten. The memory is not lost. Only the bereaved's relationship with it has changed.

How a person resolves his grief depends on many factors. Parkes lists determinants of the way resolution occurs, distinguishing among those that existed prior to the loss, those that arise during grieving, and those that exist following the grief experience:

Determinants Antecedent to the Grief Experience

Childhood experiences (especially losses of significant persons)
Later experiences (especially losses of significant persons)
Previous mental illness (especially depressive illness)
Life crisis prior to the bereavement

Relationship with the deceased
Kinship (spouse, child, parent, etc.)
Strength of attachment
Security of attachment
Degree of reliance
Intensity of ambivalence (love/hate)
Mode of death
Timeliness
Previous warnings
Preparation for bereavement
Need to hide feelings

Determinants Concurrent with the Grief Experience

Sex
Age
Personality
Grief proneness
Inhibition of feelings
Socioeconomic status (social class)
Nationality
Religion (faith and rituals)
Cultural and familial factors influencing expression of grief

Determinants Subsequent to the Grief Experience

Social support or isolation
Secondary stresses
Emergent life opportunities (options open)[52]

Bowlby lists five variables affecting the course of grief, noting that the personality of the bereaved is most important:

The identity and role of the person lost
The age and sex of the person bereaved
The causes and circumstances of the loss
The social and psychological circumstances affecting the bereaved at the time of and after the loss
The personality of the bereaved with special reference to his capacities for making love relationships and for responding to stressful situations.[53]

The course of reorganization and integration may follow any of a variety of paths. But no matter what the course is, if the griefwork is complete a strong new identity will emerge. When a person does not allow himself to experience each part of his grief, he may not be able to move on in his life.

Any one of the determinants of grieving listed above may be a factor in incomplete grieving. Another important impediment to grief resolution is society's lack of knowledge about the mourning process. Our culture is uncomfortable with strong, painful emotions, and individuals often have a misconstrued understanding of courage. Many well-intentioned friends and family support "self-control" through the suppression, delay, and displacement of grieving emotions. When this happens, grief may be unnecessarily prolonged. The deceased may become glorified. It may seem easier for the bereaved to hang on to the sorrow than to dare to face life alone or to look at other sources of life's problems. Grieving cannot be separated from other psychological processes in a person's life. If one's life is dysfunctional, his grief will be as well.

For the counselor: The primary job of the counselor is to support the emerging identity of the bereaved as well as to reassure him during any temporary regressions. The client needs to trust that he is not betraying the memory of the deceased as he moves out into a new definition of self.

If his grieving is incomplete, he should be supported in examining the possible reasons for this. More intense psychotherapy may be required if unresolved grief is affecting full functioning, and its causes are not clear.

NORMAL GRIEF AND PATHOLOGICAL GRIEF

In his classic work about the management of acute grief reactions, Erich Lindemann describes the characteristics of normal grief as "somatic distress, preoccupation with the image of the deceased, guilt, hostile reactions, and loss of patterns for conduct."[54] Schneider adds sadness, loneliness, and exhaustion.[55] These symptoms may occur in any combination and may happen immediately or be delayed, but the normal grief process does show a pattern of lessening intensity over time.

Pathological grief often does not allow for movement in the direction of reduced intensity. The normal grief reactions may be distorted, exaggerated, prolonged, inhibited, or delayed. Two of the major signs of disordered grieving are chronic mourning and prolonged absence of conscious grieving. There are often side-effects with these symptoms. Depression and disorganization may accompany chronic mourning,

TABLE 1
KEY DIFFERENCES BETWEEN
NORMAL AND PATHOLOGICAL GRIEF*

	GRIEF	PATHOLOGICAL GRIEF
Time since loss	most intense reactions are seen prior to six months	intense reactions last longer than six months with little sign of resolution
View of the loss	holding-on strategies: wants to believe the loss can be restored but knows it cannot. Reality-testing (after initial phase of shock) is intact.	continues to operate "as if" loss was still there. Chronic continuing hope for return of lost person or object. Refusal to actively reality-test.
Preoccupation	Variable: can be intensely focused on loss or able to function. Acute awareness of what happened at time of loss, emotionally, physically, and cognitively.	Active: seeking reunion with lost object or person or clear ongoing disruption and dysfunction in daily routine; acute awareness of what happened at the time of the loss is usually cognitive only.
Dreams/imagery	Manifest content of dreams is variable, but contains recognition of the absence of what has been lost.	Manifest content focused on attempts to save or destroy what was lost.
Approach/ Avoidance Behaviors	Ambivalent about dealing with loss, but willing to do so.	Avoids situations which remind bereaved of the loss.
Intellectual/ Emotional Integration	Intellectual and emotional awareness of loss.	Intellectual awareness only, or emotional awareness without linking to intellectual awareness.

*Source: J.M. Schneider, "Clinically Significant Differences Between Grief, Pathological Grief, and Depression," unpublished manuscript, Michigan State University College of Medicine, 1980, p. 19.

while illness or acute depression may be associated with the absence of conscious grief. In both types of disordered grieving the mourner has not given up the urge to search. There appears to be a lack of reality-testing: the loss feels reversible.[56]

One major difference between normal and pathological grief is the length of time over which grieving occurs. If it is episodic, it is usually healthy. Another indication of pathology is the excessive effect of the grieving on the individual's functioning. It is difficult to distinguish chronic or pathological grief in words alone. Once a counselor has had experience in the field, he will intuitively feel the difference. It is important to remember that one usually needs to see a client for a number of sessions before it can be determined whether the grief is normal or pathological, and that, because of lack of familiarity, grief can feel pathological to the client when it is really normal. Table 1 may be helpful in distinguishing normal from pathological grief.

For the counselor: The prescribed treatment for normal grief is to help the client deeply experience his loss. The client's grief itself is what requires the counselor's attention, and this suggests a therapeutic interaction quite unlike most others. There is no immediate need for "uncovering" work; it is a time for healing.

Pathological grief, on the other hand, requires more than non-professional emotional support, since intervention therapy, advice giving, and supportive confrontation may be needed. A trained therapist may be able to suggest ways of exploring blocked emotions or of closely reliving the death itself.

Professional work with clients experiencing pathological grief is not within the scope of this book. For a fuller treatment of that subject the reader is referred to the current literature on psychotherapeutic techniques.

REFERENCES

[1]B. Simos, *A Time to Grieve,* New York: Family Service of America, 1979.

[2]*Ibid.*

[3]E. Kübler-Ross, *On Death and Dying,* New York: Macmillan, 1969.

[4]A. Weisman, *On Dying and Denying,* New York: Behavioral Publications, 1972.

[5]R. Kalish, *Death, Grief, and Caring Relationships*, Monterey, Calif.: Brooks-Cole, 1981, p. 207. Quoted in Christopher News Notes #206, "Let's Talk About Death," undated, *Cadillac Evening News*, Cadillac, Michigan.

[6]Kara multimedia presentation. Created 1980 for Kara, Inc., Palo Alto, CA 94301.

[7]E. Pattison, *The Experience of Dying*, Englewood Cliffs, N.J.: Prentice-Hall, 1977.

[8]*Ibid.*, p. 47-48 paraphrase.

[9]*Supra* note 7.

[10]S. Freud, "The Future of an Illusion," in J. Strachney (ed.), *The Complete Psychological Works of Sigmund Freud*, New York: Macmillan, 1964.

[11]*Supra* note 7.

[12]I. Yalom, *Existential Psychotherapy*. New York: Basic Books, 1980.

[13]*Ibid.*, p. 120.

[14]*Ibid.*

[15]*Supra* note 7.

[16]*Supra* note 12.

[17]E. Fromm, *The Art of Loving*, New York: Harper & Row, 1956, p. 8.

[18]John J.L. Mood, (trans.) *Rilke on Love and Other Difficulties; Translations and Considerations of Rainer Maria Rilke*. New York: W.W. Norton, 1975, p. 28.

[19]E.C. Latham, (ed.) from *The Poetry of Robert Frost* "Desert Places." N.Y.: Holt, Rinehart and Winston, 1969.

[20]*Supra* note 7.

[21] C. Simonton, S. Mathews-Simonton, and J. Creighton, *Getting Well Again,* Los Angeles: J.P. Tarcher, 1978.

[22] The Center for Attitudinal Healing is at 19 Main St., Tiburon, Calif. 94920.

[23] *Supra* note 12.

[24] *Ibid.,* p. 119.

[25] *Supra* note 4.

[26] *Ibid.*

[27] R.C. Cantor, *And a Time to Live: Toward Emotional Well-Being During the Crisis of Cancer,* New York: Harper and Row, 1978.

[28] D. Larson and C. Garfield, *Berkeley Hospice Training Project,* unpublished manuscript, Berkeley Hospice Training Project, Berkeley, Calif., 1982.

[29] *Supra* note 27, p. 50.

[30] E. Stotland, *The Psychology of Hope,* San Francisco: Jossey-Bass, 1969.

[31] V. Frankl, *Man's Search For Meaning,* Boston: Beacon Press, 1963.

[32] *Supra* note 1, p. 188.

[33] *Supra* note 21.

[34] L. LeShan, "Psychotherapy and the Dying Patient," in L. Pearson (ed.), *Death and Dying,* Cleveland: Case Western Reserve Press, 1969.

[35] A.C. Carr and B. Schoenberg, "Object Loss and Somatic Symptom Formation," in B. Schoenberg *et al., Loss and Grief: Psychological Management in Medical Practice,* New York: Columbia University Press, 1970.

[36] *The Course in Miracles* (anonymous), Tiburon, Calif.: Foundation for Inner Peace, 1975.

[37]*Supra* note 7, p. 308-309.

[38]J. Hinton, "The Physiological and Mental Distress of Dying," *Quarterly Journal of Medicine,* 32:1-21, 1963; H. Lieberman, "Psychological Correlates of Impending Death," *Journal of Gerontology,* 10:181-190, 1965.

[39]*Supra* note 4.

[40]*Supra* note 7.

[41]Kalish, *supra* note 5, p. 34.

[42]*Ibid.,* p. 43.

[43]*Ibid.,* p. 45.

[44]*Ibid.*

[45]*Supra* note 4.

[46]J. Bowlby, *Attachment and Loss* (Vol. 3): *Sadness and Depression,* New York: Basic Books, 1980; Cantor, *supra* note 27; C.M. Parkes, *Bereavement Studies of Grief in Adult Life,* New York: International University Press, 1972; Simos, *supra* note 1.

[47]J. Tatelbaum, *The Courage of Grief,* New York: Harper and Row, 1980, p. 27.

[48]Kalish, *supra* note 5, p. 188.

[49]C.S. Lewis, *A Grief Observed,* New York: Seabury Press, 1961, p. 1.

[50]Bowlby, *supra* note 46.

[51]*Supra* note 49, p. 10.

[52]Parkes, *supra* note 46, p. 121.

[53]Bowlby, *supra* note 46, p. 172.

[54]E. Lindemann, "The Symptomology and Management of Acute Grief," *American Journal of Psychiatry,* 101:14-48, 1944, p. 142.

[55] J.M. Schneider, "Clinically Significant Differences Between Grief, Pathological Grief, and Depression," unpublished manuscript, Michigan State University, College of Medicine, 1980.

[56] Bowlby, *supra* note 46; R.W. Ramsey, "Behavioral Approaches to Bereavement," *Behavioral Research,* 15:131-35, 1977; Schneider, *supra* note 55.

CHAPTER FOUR

THE SEARCH FOR MEANING AND IMMORTALITY

"I am dying. There is a terrible fear and bitterness, and a sense of there not being any time to do anything; that life is all the dreams that I dreamed and is just that, just dreams. The dreams are going to go nowhere. I am not going to realize them. It is all over before I realized it started. I went around living in a dream for most of my life and all of a sudden it's all over, and I never even woke up."

—*Kara client*
A 60 year old woman
dying of cancer

Death can both destroy and create meaning. In the face of this, an individual may search for ways to insure his immortality. He will want to know he left a "mark on the world," his assurance of continuation after death through symbolic immortality. Lifton describes five ways in which an individual either seeks immortality or is confirmed that he is, in fact, immortal:

> This sense of immortality may be expressed biologically, by living on through one's sons and daughters and their sons and daughters, extending out into social dimensions (of tribe, organization, people, nation, or even species); theologically, in the idea of a life after death or of other forms of spiritual conquest of death; creatively, through "works" and influences persisting beyond biological death; naturally, through identification with nature, with its infinite extension into time and space; or transcendentally, through a feeling-state so intense that time and death disappear.[1]

Biological, creative, and natural symbols reflect the meaning a person finds in his life. The theological and transcendent aspects imply a search for the meaning of life as well as meaning or purpose in life. In these domains, we may develop a sense of how we relate to the universe and design our purpose in life according to a sense of a larger purpose.

When a Kara counselor talks to people facing death or experiencing grief, questions involving the ultimate purpose of life and the meaning they may find in their time left on earth come up often. Men and women who were once religious may now question whether there is a God. Atheists may discover a whole new spiritual truth for themselves. People who are dying may need to define clearly what they have created and given to others during their lifetime. They probably will question if they actually did what they intended to do and will look for evidence of their personal significance. They need to insure their own immortality after they are gone, as is shown in this excerpt from a letter written by a Kara client to her counselor when she found out her cancer was terminal:

> When facing the end of my life, when realizing I will die, I reach out for a way to have *me* last forever. My life seems only to be worth something if it extends over time beyond the years that I've lived it:

in a child's memory, in the knowledge of eternal life, or in a book I wrote. So, I wish I had children, or I wish I wrote that novel or I took that drug to experience the Truth about Nirvana. I want to be convinced that this is not all there is. I am going to die. Even love does not seem enough today to make my life meaningful.

The counselor's role in discussing these issues with a client is to encourage him to define his own life purpose and to think about what he feels he is leaving behind. The counselor also needs to become familiar with his own responses to these questions about life's purpose. No matter what philosophical or spiritual beliefs the counselor may hold, he must put aside his own opinions and perspectives when he pays attention to the client.

Following are more detailed descriptions of the different kinds of immortality that Lifton described: biological immortality through children, immortality through creative works, immortality through nature, theological immortality, and transcendent immortality. When facing death one may find meaning and purpose in any or all of these.

BIOLOGICAL IMMORTALITY

The production of offspring is an obvious way to achieve a kind of immortality both genetically and through the vast influence a parent has on the growth of a child. Through children one is connected both forward and backward in time, a part of the unbroken chain of individual lives that makes up the human race:

> As long as your descendants continue to have children and as long as humanity exists, some part of you continues ... Our present life thus becomes one existence in a series of existences, and we are part of the series rather than simply an isolated life. The series stretches far back in time and also will stretch far forward in time.[2]

This kind of immortality has a social dimension as well. An individual has an historical connection with his family name, roots, tribe, nationality, or other group he identifies with. To the degree he sees these groups representing who he is, he will be immortal. He will also exist in the memories of those whom he has encountered in his life: family, friends, and colleagues.

Another aspect of biological immortality is seen in the concern for physical prolongation of life. History has continually been influenced by those searching for eternal life. Most people believe that proper health practices will extend life, but not insure eternal life. Still, people often seem to assume that if a person eats well, exercises, and lives with the right beliefs, he will live forever. The belief that there must be a "good enough" life to insure immortality may derive from the story of Adam and Eve, who could have lived forever if they had not sinned. Evidence of this belief is found in the person who, observing that an acquaintance has died, concludes: "Of course the man had a heart attack. Smoking two packs a day, drinking like a fish, and working twelve hours a day to pile up the dollars: he was just asking for it."[3] The implication is that if the observer does not smoke or drink or work too hard, he may escape his own mortality.

Another controversial way a person may attempt to insure physical immortality is through cryogenics. This is a practice in which the body is frozen at the moment of death—to be thawed when a cure for the disease which caused death is found.

This raises the ethical question of when death actually occurs. A person can be alive, but totally dependent on mechanical life-support systems. This will not insure immortality, but will prolong biological life. A client may want to explore these questions if life-support systems are likely to be recommended. The counselor needs to inform the family about options, including a living will which states that the patient wants no artificial interventions to prolong his life. The family and patient may need help in clarifying their wishes in this matter.

IMMORTALITY THROUGH CREATIVE WORKS

In addition to the creation of children, the creation of something that will continue to live on insures symbolic immortality.

> ... every act of ours, the moment it is realized, is disjoined from us and living an immortal life of its own; and since we are nothing else in reality than the series of our acts, we too are immortal, for to have lived once is to live forever.[4]

The achievement of immortality through "works" is intimately connected to a person's desire for meaning and purpose. There is a difference between "work" and "works." *Work* is what a person does in order to survive; works are created from an intention or purpose, with the desire for fulfillment.[5] Work may or may not involve the creation of works.

There is a growing movement in our culture to have work that fills survival needs be a source of significant works, to have less alienation between a person and what he does to make a living. *Works* may mean planting a garden that will continue to grow, developing a business, writing a book, creating an artistic project, or any other outward expression of the self. Works could also be extended to mean the acquisition of land or property that will be passed on to future generations. This includes trusts and endowments. There is a sense of identity and accomplishment in these works, and a feeling of satisfaction from the knowledge that the person will not be forgotten after death.

Many bereaved take comfort in the works of the deceased, which are a reminder that the person did exist and was appreciated by others. But while focusing on such reminders provides a sense of continuity with the loved one, this may create difficulties if the bereaved does not eventually move on to develop a separate identity. Creating works of one's own also may help the grieving survivor to find new meaning in his or her life. A Kara client who had lost her husband seemed to have lost her sense of purpose as well. She had idolized her husband and built her life around him. Yet in spite of her deep grief, she continued her newly begun pursuit at a nursing career. A year and a half later, discussing her grieving process, she described her nursing career as giving her the sense of purpose in life she had lost with her husband's death. In this case immersion in work did not help the client to avoid her grief, though many people do use their work to shield themselves from the pain of loss.

IMMORTALITY THROUGH NATURE

The identification with nature as a confirmation of immortality is different from creating progeny or works. The individual does not actively engage in anything, but merely uses nature to recognize his own place in the larger scheme of things.

A ten-year-old child told her counselor that death was like nature. She said that when she dies, she will be buried and all the different parts of her will go into the earth. Then, eventually, she would help a flower or a tree to grow, and in this way, she would return to live in a new form. This explanation focused only on what would happen to her body, but it also implied the continuation of her energy. She was proud of the fact that she would be a part of nature after she died and seemed quite at peace with the idea of her death.

Identification with nature is perhaps more common among people who lack strong religious beliefs or feel there is no continuation of the individual soul after death. There is some consolation in the fact that physical energy does not disappear from the universe, but only changes in form. Ruth Moro describes her experience with nature as a healing force in her grief after her husband's suicide:

I gravitated toward nature as a source of spiritual comfort. The extremes of my spirit were trying and fatiguing. These, combined with the intensities of my psychological and emotional experiences, were somehow soothed in a comforting peace as I joined with nature's beauty. I felt like the tearful child whose wretched sobs are comforted by Mother's embrace. I was very aware of nature's touch upon me: of the skies resting on my shoulders and moving in and out through my skin and lungs; of the gently intimate infiltration of the birds' songs and scratchings; of the might of crashing waves. With my eyes I felt nature's beauty as a visual stroke upon my soul. Time spent in nature was time spent developing an awareness of a greater physical self with whom I was bonded and, indeed, of whom I was an expression. The avenue of this growing awareness was the soothing peace that was nature's effect on my being.[6]

If a client speaks of nature as an important element in his life, the counselor should consider exposing him to nature in any way he can. One counselor took her client along with his oxygen on weekly rides into the country until he became too sick to go. Another counselor brought books of the Himalayan mountains to his client and watched slide shows of the client's own mountain treks.

One final example of how nature affects grief is seen in the following description of an experience with a Kara client who had lost her husband in a boating accident. Her husband had been sailing with his uncle when the boat capsized. The husband panicked and was held afloat by his uncle, but the uncle finally had to let go of his nephew when they both began to drown. Later the drowned man's wife was watching a television show about how kangaroo babies, blind and tiny, have to crawl to the mother's pouch. If the baby drops off, the mother does not pick it up. It is left to die. It was inconceivable to the client that the mother would not pick up the baby. She struggled with this, returning again and again to the uncle's decision to let go of her husband. She described to her counselor the feeling she had inside of giving up when faced with what she called "the survival of the fittest" and the seeming indifference of nature to the question of who lives and who dies.

THEOLOGICAL IMMORTALITY

Different religions describe what happens after death in different ways. As a result, some people believe in reincarnation, others in the resurrection of the soul into Christ; still others say that the soul simply moves on and joins the eternal. There are those, too, who say that the question is irrelevant and unanswerable. In any case, this has been one of the central issues of importance to mankind throughout the ages.

Religion is believed to have a critical influence on the course of dying or grieving. Augustine and Kalish interviewed doctors, nurses, and hospital chaplains about the most important factors in an "appropriate" death. They found that recognizing meaning in the life that had been lived, finding meaning in the lives that remained, and recognizing a sense of continuity or immortality were the most important factors.[7] They also interviewed clergy who work with the dying about the influence of religion on dying. The clergy all agreed that religion played an important role in coping with dying, but that intimate relationships were the most important supportive factor. Anxiety was diminished for patients who had someone with whom to discuss their dying. Often the family, nurses, and other medical staff could not be available, so an outside friend or counselor filled that role. Religion entered as the patient searched for the meaning of his death and life. Few religious conversations were about the philosophy of religion. Most were about the "awareness of being loved and related to, whether the giver of love was the symbolic value of a loving God, or of Christ triumphant, or of a loving friend or relative."[8] Finding meaning through loving relationships can be easily interpreted as religious as well as psychological in nature.

The experience of religion is more important than the specific form that religiousness takes. Augustine and Kalish note that there are three important considerations in supporting a person who is dying:

> (1) open communication concerning dying between patients and intimates, (2) physical and psychic closeness in these relationships, and (3) [discussion of] specifically religious beliefs. A deep awareness of death, intimate verbal and non-verbal sharing, and commonly understood doctrinal beliefs, seem to bear a close phenomenological resemblance to each other. All of these relate to perceiving meaning in life and in self, which can be a transcendent religious experience, given a definition of religion that is not restrictive.[9]

The act of counseling a dying client can itself be a spiritual experience. Paying close attention to another human being often creates the experience of unconditional love that can be similar to the religious experience of God.

The language of the dying patient may be traditionally religious or individual and personal. It takes an attentive listener to discern the subjective feeling states and to talk about meaning in the patient's life with the appropriate metaphor. The symbols of formal religion are valuable, but acknowledgment of the personal symbols and experiences more common in the Western world are equally meaningful. These less formal personal symbols are not common currency, so the counselor must be comfortable with intimate communication and able to listen attentively. Knowledge of religious belief systems can provide only partial aid in supporting a dying client, the most important requirement being attentiveness and sensitivity to the client's communication style and the ability to respond appropriately. With this caution in mind, we will briefly review some of the beliefs and symbols of the two major Western religions as a guide to counselors who may work with traditionally religious clients.

The Jewish Tradition

The Jewish tradition has not developed a set theory about the afterlife. The focus is on life in this world with the understanding that with death, the body returns to the earth and the soul moves on. There is a traditional story of Ba'al Shem holding two notes in his pocket. One says: "For dust you are, and to dust you shall return." The other says: "You are created in the image of God." In other words, the body may be mortal, but the soul is eternal.

At the moment of death, the dying person should have the words of his morning prayer on his lips, "The Lord our God is one." And in the traditional family, one of the immediate relatives should tear his or her garment, marking the beginning of mourning.[10] The Orthodox family may cover all the mirrors in the house in order to de-emphasize adornment of the body while the body of the dead one is present. The dead body is not left alone before the burial. Immediately after the death, members of the Orthodox Jewish community will perform Taharah, the ritual washing of the dead. This washing used to occur in pure springs or streams, but now occurs at the temple or funeral home.

The Jewish tradition sees every person as equal in death, so the burial is simple. The body is often wrapped in plain white shrouds and prayer shawls, and the casket is traditionally a plain wooden one. The burial is meant to support the natural decomposition of the body and its return to the earth. The funeral usually occurs twenty-four hours after the death, with no outsiders present. This is the time for the immediate family to express their pain and grief.

During the burial service, the coffin is placed in the grave with the words, "May he come to his place in peace." After that, family members drop a few handfuls of earth on the coffin, to insure recognition that the death has occurred. The mourners remain until the coffin is fully covered, which further underscores the finality of the death.

After the burial, the neighbors and friends bring over a "meal of consolation" to the mourning family. Eggs are often included in the meal, representing fertility and the "round wheel of fate."[11] This meal marks the beginning of the seven-day period of Shivah. All bereaved are expected to drop their regular life tasks and to participate fully in this period of mourning. It is a time for family members to grieve, talk to relatives, and be comforted.

The tradition during Shivah is not to approach the bereaved family member until he talks first, which fits the needs of a bereaved person extremely well. The wanting to be with others but not to talk is described by C.S. Lewis after his wife died.

> There is a sort of invisible blanket between the world and me. I find it hard to take in what anyone says. Or perhaps, hard to want to take it in. It is so uninteresting. Yet I want the others to be around me. I dread the moments when the house is empty. If only they would talk to one another and not to me.[12]

After the Shivah there are thirty days of mourning when the bereaved may return to work but his other social activities are restricted. When the mourning is for parents, these restrictions last one year.

After one year there is an unveiling of the tombstone and a ceremony of lighting a twenty-four hour candle to mark the memory of the dead. Every year after that a twenty-four hour candle is lit, and there is a prayer for the person's soul and a reaffirmation of the presence of God.

The form of ritual expression in Judaism is often the same no matter how traditional a person is. It is the understanding of the ritual that varies. What is consistent is the belief in the oneness of God and the unknown quality of the afterlife. The Jewish tradition recognizes immortality mainly through children and the memories of family and friends. The goal is to live with love and with God in the heart and to be as authentically oneself as possible. It is important for the counselor to consult with the patient and his rabbi to determine how the rituals of his dying and burial are to be performed.

The Christian Religion

Christianity originated in the death and resurrection of Christ. The traditional Christian recognizes two deaths: physical death, or the end to biological life, and mystical death, which is victory over physical death and sin followed by resurrection to eternal life with Christ.[13] Resurrection symbolizes the coming together of what a person is and what he could become. Death is no longer dreaded, but seen as an opportunity to live eternally with God.

The purpose of life for a Christian is to love God with all his being and to love his neighbor as himself. That will not be perfectly achieved in this life, and many Christians believe that beyond death is further opportunity to realize that goal.

Some Christians believe that after death there is a final judgment, at which it is determined whether the individual has lived a responsible life and fulfilled his potential. If he has, he can enter the Kingdom of God. This judgment can be difficult for a dying Christian who questions the value of his life, feels guilty, and is afraid of being judged.

Death is the gateway to eternal life, but there is a wide variety in Christian perspectives on sin and judgment, heaven and hell, and the ultimate benevolence of God. Traditionally, the viewpoint was that all human beings are sinners, and death is a punishment for sin. Funerals traditionally have been black and somber. Currently, there is a trend toward celebrating the resurrection of the dead person into Christ. The clergy may wear white and acknowledge the pain and loss of the bereaved, as well as emphasize the death as the last stage of growth towards God.

Each Christian church has its own rites of passage and rites of burial. These are occasions for the expression of faith and hope in God, thanksgiving for and remembrance of the deceased, communal sharing and support, and public recognition that death has occurred. Unlike the Jewish tradition, where the rituals are more cross-cultural, in the Christian tradition the rituals of death are closely related to the larger culture. For example, in Latin America there are nine days of feasting and prayers after the funeral, and there is much open expression of grief and other emotions.[14] In North America, the funeral rituals, as well as the emotional expressions, are usually more restrained.

If the counselor finds himself in a situation where religion is very important to the dying or grieving person, prayer can be effective. Reading from the Bible or other religious tracts also may be supportive. The Psalms, especially the twenty-third (about going through the Valley of Death), are good resources for biblical prayer. There is also another New Testament prayer that has been found useful in working with children. It is Mark 10:13-16, in which Jesus gives a beautiful greeting to the children and invites them to come to him.

Prayer and ritual often unlock deep emotions and take people to the depths of reality in a way that nothing else can. Dr. John Golenski, a Jesuit priest, describes an incident in which religious ritual became the only way to communicate with a woman who had just lost her child. The child had been beaten severely and the mother was hysterical, refusing to believe he was dead. Dr. Golenski soon realized that, in this case,

101

talking would have no effect. He donned his vestments and began prayers for the salvation of her son. After a while the mother broke down and cried, acknowledging the death through this symbolic and ritual act.[15]

A counselor who does not have spiritual training obviously could not do what Golenski did, but could respond in any symbolic way that is comfortable. Supporting the client in reaching out to his own church may be the most appropriate role a counselor could play in this situation.

One of our clients shared a profound period at the end of his life with his Kara counselor. Howard was eighty years old and a minister. He had committed his life to probing its meaning and had studied many religions. He had books and relics from all over the world, and his books were marked throughout with dates, questions, and notes from the many times he had read them. Howard was a seeker, and this last search was for some proof that he had learned it well enough to insure that he would die in the arms of God. Towards the end of his journey he brought his Kara counselor along, spending many weeks planning what he wanted her to read to him during the moments of his death. Yet, at the same time, another part of him was resisting death. It was difficult for him to let go of his possessions, and for months he asked his counselor to hold boxes for him until he knew whom he wanted to have them. Then he would ask her to bring certain books or notes back so he could share ideas with her.

As time went on, Howard was in great pain and spent more time worrying about his bodily needs than his spiritual concerns. In his last month he began to withdraw and to sulk occasionally. He would not call his counselor, waiting for her to call and show she cared. They still had moments of deep spiritual connection, but much less often than before.

In the end, he died alone in the hospital. The day before, when his counselor had visited, he seemed to be deep inside himself. The nurse aroused him. He looked at his counselor and said, "I'll see you again." She returned the next day and found him on his side, his breathing labored. He did not open his eyes and did not make any other contact. His counselor held his hand thinking, "It's O.K., Howard, death is part of life." Repeatedly, as she thought those words, his whole body would jerk. The counselor continued to think, "It's natural to die. Go in peace." She sat for a while longer, then half an hour after she left, Howard died. It was not how he said he wanted it, but he might have been pleased to know that when his counselor was told he died she immediately sat down and read the readings he had put together. As she was reading, she realized what Howard had gathered together was not for himself but for her, the survivor.

Studies of anxiety and fear of death in people who are religious, atheistic, and agnostic have found that both the deeply religious and deeply irreligious have the least fear. Those who are unsure show the greatest fear.[16] Many of the clients a counselor will encounter do not have a clear understanding of their own spiritual beliefs, the meaning of life, or what happens after death. Yet, each client faces these issues at least unconsciously.

There are clients who cannot easily accept the traditional symbols of religion and believe the religious solution is an avoidance. In the face of death, these people may think that there is nothing to hold on to, and thus they experience despair and a desire for certainty and resolution. Yet some may be able to tolerate this ambiguity and feel that the act of not accepting "easy answers" is a courageous one. With exposure to a variety of religious and nonreligious beliefs, a counselor will gain the ability to maintain a flexible attitude about these issues with each client. There are several good books that will help.[17]

TRANSCENDENT IMMORTALITY

The final approach to immortality, that of experiential transcendence, differs from the others in being a psychic state.[18] It refers to a mystical sense of oneness with the universe that may come not only with a religious experience, but also "in song, dance, battle, sexual love, childbirth, athletic effort, mechanical flight, or in contemplative works of artists or intellectual creation."[19] The transcendent experience enables the individual to feel a sense of unity with perceptual intensity and reorders reality so that he emerges a different person. This is the essential death-rebirth experience.

Transcendence, in the present context, means the transformation of perception so that the emotional and philosophical difficulties death presents are overcome. While the facts of reality are not changed, perception is so altered that the quality and significance of those facts are changed.[20]

Many people believe that man has a higher or transcendent nature, which is a part of his biological nature as a species. This transcendent aspect of our nature is experienced in what Maslow has called "peak" or religious experiences.[21] The peak experience is encountered in some form by most people at some time in their lives. It can come during childbirth, at someone's deathbed, while one is experiencing a natural event at the ocean or in the mountains, through drugs, or in psychosis. It can also come from meditation or from a deep personal encounter with another human being.

In the transcendent or peak experience there is often a clear perception that the universe is of one piece and eternal. Each individual has a place in it. With this view, the world, people, and external objects can be perceived more objectively. During a peak experience a person may feel larger, stronger, expanded, more tolerant and loving. He may transcend his ego and appear selfless, without personal desires and describe himself as connected with all the rest of existence. There is often a disorientation in time and space as well. The emotions of awe, humility, oneness and surrender are common. The routine problems of life fall into perspective and seem resolved or transcended. Often, death is no longer feared. In fact, most anxieties, fears, and confusions become less intense.

The Moment of Death

The moment of death is believed to be for some a transcendent experience. Certainly not everyone experiences death this way, but the phenomenon appears to be common enough to warrant exploration.

Information about the experience of the moment of death has been gathered from people who have had near-death experiences. The first formal presentation of the near-death experience was made by Albert Hein, who lived through a near-fatal fall in the Alps in the late 1800s, and later interviewed other survivors of near-fatal accidents, especially falls while mountain climbing. He found that in 95 percent of the cases people had experiences similar to his: an altered state of reality where time and space were expanded, great clarity of mind, and often a "life review" process. The emotional tone of the experience was one of peace and harmony.[22]

Russel Noyes defines three stages that dying patients commonly experience: resistance to dying; life-review; and transcendence, or a feeling of peace and expansion into the universe. All patients do not go through all three stages. Some stop at stage one, and others at stage two.[23] Resistance comes with the recognition that death is imminent. There ensues a brief struggle, often accompanied by anxiety. Noyes sees the struggle here between the surge of life-saving energy and the urge to surrender. When surrendering finally occurs, a feeling of tranquility may develop. There is sometimes a splitting of the self from the body, referred to as an "out of body" experience, when the patient objectively observes himself from above the bed or across the room.

At this point, a life review can take place. This is usually a series of vivid scenes of the important events in the dying person's life. The review of early memories is a kind of grieving as the patient clings to that which tells him who he is. As Noyes describes it, "life arises to a sharper focus and is clung to as more precious just at the moment it is about to be lost."[24]

The individual may then move into the phase of transcendence, a non-temporal state. He may see his whole life simultaneously and become aware of a change in his relationship with time—as if he is outside the past and future, in eternity. He transcends his individual identity and the experience of space as well. This results in a sense of oneness with the universe, often accompanied by a sense of truth. The patient may intuitively find the answer to the question, "Who am I?" Loss of control or a feeling of surrendering to a larger will is another characteristic of this phase, along with ecstasy or great calm.

Ray Moody, Jr., in his book *Life After Life,* presents a classic description of the moment-of-death experience. His patients, who were pronounced clinically dead and were then revived, described the altered state of floating outside their bodies with a feeling of peace. Most of them felt themselves moving through a tunnel with some ethereal being at the other end to greet them and help them through the transition. Often the dying came to a turning point when they were told to return to their bodies, which usually was met with resistance and sadness at having to go back. On return to the body, these people's lives were profoundly changed, especially their relationships with death.[25]

Garfield studied transcendent experiences in dying patients rather than in individuals who survived the experience of near-death. He found that 21 percent of the 173 cancer patients he interviewed had transcendent experiences, which fell into four categories. Some patients perceived a white light, heard music, and saw a figure (either a religious figure or a relative) beckoning to them. They described the experience as "real, peaceful, and beautiful." Other patients experienced demons with a great sense of clarity and reality. Still others had vivid images that were both peaceful and demonic. And some patients experienced a void or a dark tunnel.[26]

Garfield also interviewed seventy-two patients in intensive care or coronary care and found that they did not have totally peace-filled visions either. One-half of the altered states reported by these patients near the end of their lives included traumatic visions. He noted that, as in psychedelic experiences, the environment seemed to influence the content of the visions in the dying patient. A supportive and loving environment was more likely to influence a peaceful experience of dying.[27]

Garfield questions the wisdom of believing that these experiences prove life after death exists. These experiences may simply be commonly shared altered states. Proposing the idea of "life after death" could serve as one more rationalization for avoiding acceptance of death and the realization of the pain and loss involved.

There is much controversy about the nature of these transcendental visions and sensations. Will a disciplined lifestyle of meditation or the practice of self-transcendence influence the experience of death? Or does everyone experience this altered state at death anyway? Does what people do with their lives influence what happens after death? Does it matter what word is on a person's lips at the moment of death? Does the experience of being one with the universe reflect reality, or is it the product of a chemical or nervous hallucination? Perhaps it does not matter, so long as it affects the individual's attitude by "removing the many artificial divisions which people impose upon the world."[28]

There are striking similarities between these subjective descriptions of the moment of death and those found in the various books written to guide the dead in the journey of the soul that is believed by many cultures to follow death. The *Tibetan Book of the Dead,* a guide book for a teacher to accompany a person in his dying, says that at the moment of death a state called a "swoon" begins, when the "clear Light of the Void"appears. If the dying person in life has practiced developing the courage to merge with the vast intensity and power of this light, he will be liberated from the cycle of repeated incarnations. Part of what is practiced in life is to be fully conscious during the moment of death.[29]

If the individual does not liberate himself to the first clear light, he begins to recognize that he is dead. This occurs as he watches his past life, starting with the vision of his own death and moving backwards in time. He may first see the room where he died and the people who were there. The *Tibetan Book of the Dead* describes this life review as a secondary way to experience the clear light, by reviewing past illusions and actions. These reviews are vividly colored and include sound and light rays as well as archetypal fantasy-forms. (Similar visions have been reported during psychedelic hallucinations or psychosis.) After this, if liberation has not been achieved, many kinds of deities, both peaceful and wrathful, appear to the dead person.[30]

If the person misses the opportunities offered for liberation again, he enters the stage of rebirth. The person's past life will determine how this stage is experienced. If he was moral, there may be happiness here. If he was immoral, he will be attacked and ravaged. His task at this level is to recognize that these are all projections of his own mind and are essentially illusions. If liberation does not occur then, he will be reborn again, and all that the book can do is guide him on what form to take for the return to life.

There are many other books of the dead, including the Egyptian, Buddhist, Moslem, Hindu, and Chinese.[31] Western cultures refer to the

Ars Moriendi (The Art of Dying), written during the Middle Ages.[32] This book served two purposes: to guide people on the dying journey and to express the importance of death in life. Most medieval death manuals agree that it is essential to create the right disposition and right attitude in dying. One must not instill false hopes of recovery. All possible support should be given to the dying to help them face death and accept it. "Courageous confrontation of death is seen as crucial; avoidance and reluctance to surrender are considered two of the major dangers the dying person faces."[33]

The central idea of these ancient texts is that it is essential for people to confront the fact of their own impermanence, since as a result they will be able to experience that element within themselves that is indestructible and immortal within their own lifetimes.[34] Stephen LeVine has oriented his work to this goal, helping dying clients who have chosen to use the dying process as a path towards transcendence.

> [Participants] ... often begin by investigating the psychological elements, the contents of the mind. And, to a certain degree, that seems useful ... as they penetrate more deeply into their being, their priorities change. They start to relate to the mind instead of from it, which allows a whole new dimension of participation in being, in life itself. They come to the edge of the mind. They see that they are none of the objects of thought or mood. They begin to relate to the light by which all this mind-stuff is seen. They come to recognize that they are awareness itself, beyond any model of solidity or expectation. They no longer confuse the light of awareness for the objects which reflect the light in the silent "I am" of the mind, consciousness itself is revealed. And they no longer mistake themselves for the objects of awareness, but instead recognize themselves as the vast space of awareness itself. *They have touched the deathless.*[35]

The transcendent experience seems to occur when the individual's identification shifts to a more universal understanding of the self as a formless process of energy. Many people have caught a glimpse of this formless place, but are afraid to substitute such nothingness for their personal identification.

> When I begin to realize that my truest identity is as process and not as fixed substance, I am on the verge of a terrible emptiness and miraculous freedom. The nothingness of being, the transitoriness of substance, the endless possibilities of awareness are so shocking to

recognize that often the sensations are those of vertigo, anxiety, and denial . . .

Very well, I can see that I am not this body, these habits I've built up, or even my profession or my family relationships. I can see that each of those parts of what I've always thought of as my identity could be replaced by quite other parts. I could have a female body instead of my man's shape; could have developed quite other ways of talking and even thinking; could have gone into another field of work or married differently, of course. But if I think, not of replacing each of these with something else, but of relinquishing all such parts of who I am without any substitution, then . . . Then . . . Then I am frightened and clawing at the walls of my nothingness, whimpering before the impassivity of silence.[36]

Practicing Transcendence and Dying

LeVine says we must practice achieving transcendence throughout our lives in order for it to affect the moment of death. Contrary to popular fantasy, total surrender to the vastness usually does not occur in the last twenty minutes of one's life.

When we think of our death we imagine ourselves surrounded by loving friends, the room filled with serene quietude that comes from nothing more to say, all business is finished. Our eyes shining with love and with a whisper of profound wisdom as to the transiency of life, we settle back into the pillow, the last breath escaping like a vast "Ahhh!" as we depart gently into the light.

But what if just as you are about to "Ahhh!" out of the body, your mate turns to you and confesses they have been having an affair with your best friend? Or your angry child comes bursting into the room saying "You've always been a jerk, why don't you stop playing games?" Would your heart slam shut like a stone door, would your mind whirl with confusion and self-doubt, would you need to say something in return to try to defend yourself, would you contract in painful agreement?

How can we die in wholeness, when we have lived our lives in such partiality? When we have lived our lives so much in the mind's precious idea of itself, how can we die with our hearts wide open to the mystery of it all? Where will we take refuge? Where will the confidence in the perfection of the moment come from when we have so often pulled back from what we feared?[37]

It seems that a variety of transcendent experiences may allow a person to "die before he dies" and thus change both the way he lives and the way he relates to death. Most people will have to undergo such an experience many times if they are to incorporate it into their world view. But the experience really needs to happen only once if it is fully experienced at the time.

> In other words, there is a certain way of facing and encountering death that has to be done only once. If a person goes through it when he is fifteen, he will not have to do it when he is seventy. This is how I understand the basic function of all the ancient temple mysteries and the primitive rites of passage that focus on the death/rebirth experience. They create a framework in which people can go through the experience of psychological annihilation and transcendence, so that from then on they will live in a psychologically different world, where life and death are sort of dialectically interrelated. Death will then have a very different meaning than it has for a person who is totally immersed in the materialistic way of looking at things.[38]

Grof conducted a study using psychedelic drugs with cancer patients, finding that the experience of death and rebirth changed a person's concept of death. The psychedelic sessions shifted the focus from goal-oriented achievement and materialism to the importance of the present moment, and patients often developed a new view about the meaning of existence. Their "peak" experiences were similar to those reported by people who have experienced near-death.[39]

For the Counselor: It is important for the counselor to recognize that this whole area of communication with clients is delicate and must be addressed with great sensitivity. The effects of psychosis, grief reactions, and para-normal experiences may be described in a similar manner, yet each requires an entirely different counseling approach. It may be difficult to determine whether an experience a client reports is a part of the normal grieving process, a genuine transcendent experience, or a sign of serious illness. There may be times when consultation with a professional therapist is indicated.

Working with a dying patient can be a reminder of the ever-changing nature of life, and it sometimes creates a transcendent experience. Here is part of what a Kara counselor wrote after an experience at a deathbed.

We'd never met before the last hour and a half of his life. Yet as soon as I walked into the room, I felt as if we'd known each other always. We should have been strangers, but we weren't. He was pan-humanity to me.

I was so grateful to him because he allowed me to share with him his last moments. He let me see, so starkly, that our true nature is not our physical body—that there is more to a human being than mere flesh. How could it be that he could physically look so ill and yet all I felt and saw was love? I learned again that we should not judge people by how they look but should strive to know them in the truest sense we can.

I saw that all of us are unified together as human beings, not just on this earth plane, but in our souls. I saw this, not through knowing R. in his life, but by sharing the time of his death with him.[40]

EFFECTS OF THE NUCLEAR AGE ON CONCEPTS OF IMMORTALITY

Freud saw ideas of immortality as representing the defense mechanisms of denial and compensation and urged people to face death openly.[41] Jung, on the other hand, noted that choosing to believe in our own immortality makes our lives more manageable.[42]

Yet it seems that we do not choose whether to believe in immortality or to see death as a final and unmitigated end. Under normal conditions the human unconscious is ambivalent about its own mortality. We know we will die, but we do not act accordingly. This is not just denial of the facts; the sense that we will not disappear from the face of the earth stems from a deep-seated connection between the individual and the human race, both forward and backward in time.[43]

In recent times, however, all this has changed. The potential for nuclear holocaust has radically altered mankind's relationship with the future and with the past. The nuclear age has presented us with new and powerful images that undermine our most basic notions of immortality. The possibility of a fatal auto accident does not pose a similar threat, since one's family, religion, works, and nature—all sources of symbolic immortality—survive and persist. But with nuclear weapons everything could be annihilated.

There are two major human responses to the loss of faith in symbolic immortality. One is to step up the search for experiential transcendence, a quest undertaken with increased urgency by many people in this country today. Another response is what has been called "psychic numbing," which occurs when what is experienced cannot be adequately expressed in individual and communal images or activity.[44]

Psychic numbing is not a conscious decision to remain indifferent; it is a psychic defense against despair. It deadens the experience of terror, anger, and grief, but at the same time it stifles creativity and keeps us from feeling fully alive. That more and more people are suffering from this modern malaise was most evident in the anti-nuclear demonstrations in June 1982 in New York City and San Francisco. In both cities there were thousands of demonstrators, but those who were there observed less chanting and singing, less camaraderie, and much less energy and activity than at rallies held in the 1960s.

We must overcome this psychic numbing if we are to again be and feel fully alive, but the despair it masks cannot be banished by "positive thinking" or artificial optimism:

> "Like grief, it must be worked through. It must be named and validated as a healthy, normal human response to the planetary situation. Faced and experienced, despair can be used: as the psyche's defenses drop away, new energies are released.[45]

We all must begin to mourn the loss of immortality that has come with the new age, acknowledge our despair, and together create new images of the future. Undertaking this task will be even more urgent for those who work with the dying and grieving for two reasons: they will be dealing with clients who are facing death without the assurance of symbolic immortality; and they need to be fully alive and in touch with their own feelings as they do so.

REFERENCES

[1]R. Lifton, "The Struggle for Cultural Rebirth," in S. Wilcox and M. Sutton, *Understanding Death and Dying,* Palo Alto, Calif.: Mayfield Publications, 1981, p. 207.

[2]R. Kalish, *Death, Grief, and Caring Relationships,* Monterey, Calif.: Brooks/Cole, 1981, p. 56.

[3]*Ibid.,* p. 58.

[4]J. Choron, *Modern Man and Mortality,* New York: Macmillan, 1964, p. 16.

[5]*Supra* note 2.

[6]R. Moro, *Death, Grief, and Widowhood,* Berkeley, Calif.: Parallax Press, 1979, p. 83-84.

[7]R. Augustine and R. Kalish, "Religion, Transcendence, and Appropriate Death," *Journal of Transpersonal Psychology* 7: 1-13, 1975.

[8]*Ibid.* p. 4.

[9]*Ibid.* p. 8.

[10]R. Siegel, M. Strassfeld, and J. Strassfeld, *The Jewish Catalogue,* Philadelphia: Jewish Publication Society of America, 1973, p. 173.

[11]*Ibid.*

[12]C.S. Lewis, *A Grief Observed,* New York: Bantam, 1961, p. 1.

[13]H. Smith, *The Religions of Man,* New York: Harper and Row, 1955.

[14]Luis Jansen, personal communications. California Institute of Transpersonal Psychology, Menlo Park, Ca., February 1983.

[15]J. Golenski, Ph.D., personal communication at Kara, 457 Kingsley Ave., Palo Alto, Ca. 94301, 1983.

[16]G. Gorer, *Death, Grief, and Mourning,* New York: Anchor Books, 1967; J. Hinton, "The Physical and Mental Distress of the Dying," *Quarterly Journal of Medicine,* 32:1-21, 1963; R. Kalish, "An Approach to the Study of Death Attitudes," *American Behavioral Scientist* 6: 68-70, 1963.

[17]Descriptions of the religious beliefs, practices, and rituals of caring for the dying of twenty-seven different faiths are provided in D.M. LeMaire (ed.), *Illness Until Death,* Kansas City, MO.: Kansas City Hospice, 1981. Another resource: J.H. Hicks, *Death and Eternal Life,* San Francisco: Harper and Row, 1976.

[18]*Supra* note 1.

[19]R. Lifton, "The Sense of Immortality: On Death and the Continuity of Life," in H. Feifel (ed.), *New Meanings of Death,* New York: McGraw-Hill, 1977, p. 279.

[20]D. Klass and A. Gordon, "Varieties of Transcending Experience at Death: A Videotape-Based Study," *Omega Journal*, 9(1): 19-36, 1978.

[21]A. Maslow, *Religions, Values, and Peak Experiences*, New York: Viking Press, 1970.

[22]A. Hein, "The Experience of Dying From Falls," (R. Noyes and R. Kletti, translators), *Omega Journal*, 3:45, 1972.

[23]R. Noyes, "Dying and Mystical Consciousness," *Journal of Thanatology*, 1:25, 1971.

[24]*Ibid.*

[25]R. Moody, *Life After Life*, New York: Bantam Books, 1975.

[26]C. Garfield, "The Dying Patient's Concern with 'Life After Death'," in R. Kastenbaum (ed.), *Between Life and Death*, New York: Springer, 1979.

[27]C. Garfield, "Dying and Death," in A. Hastings, J. Fadiman, and J. Gordon (eds.), *Health for the Whole Person*, Boulder, Colo.: Westview Press, 1980.

[28]S. Grof, "Transitions, Birth, Death, and Rebirth," in S. Grof, H. Cayce, and P. Johnson, *Dimensions of Dying and Rebirth*, Virginia Beach, Va.: A.R.E. Books, 1977.

[29]W.E. Evans-Wentz (trans.), *The Tibetan Book of the Dead*, London: Oxford University Press, 1960.

[30]*Ibid.*

[31]S. Grof and C. Grof, *Beyond Death*, New York: Thames and Hudson, 1980.

[32]R. Rainer, "Ars Moriendi," in S. Grof and C. Grof, *Ibid.*

[33]*Supra* note 31, p. 19.

[34]S. Grof, *Realms of the Human Unconscious*, New York: Viking Press, 1975.

[35]S. LeVine, *Who Dies?* Garden City, N.Y.: Anchor Press/Doubleday, 1982, p. 61.

[36]J. Bugental, *Psychotherapy and Process,* Menlo Park, Calif.: Addison-Wesley, 1978, p. 133-134.

[37]*Supra* note 35, p. 8.

[38]*Supra* note 34, p. 70.

[39]*Ibid.*

[40]Marsha Clark, Kara counselor, written at Kara, 457 Kingsley Ave. Palo Alto, Ca. 94301.

[41]J. Strachney (ed.), *The Complete Psychological Works of Sigmund Freud,* New York: Macmillan, 1964.

[42]C. Jung, *Memories, Dreams, and Reflections* (A. Jaffee, trans.), New York: Random House, 1962.

[43]*Supra* note 19.

[44]*Ibid.*

[45]J.R. Macy, "How to Deal with Despair," *New Age Journal,* June, 40-45, 1979.

APPLICATIONS AND SKILLS

INTRODUCTION TO PART II

Counseling the dying and grieving is unlike other forms of therapy in that it usually relies less on intervention with a goal of psychotherapeutic change and more on the counselor's ability to listen carefully and relate to the client without imposing his or her own values and expectations.

> Those who can sit in silence with their fellow man, not knowing what to say, but knowing that they should be there, can bring new life into a dying heart. Those who are not afraid to hold a hand in gratitude, to shed tears in grief, and to let a sigh of distress arise straight from the heart can break through paralyzing boundaries, and witness the birth of a new fellowship, the fellowship of the broken.[1]

Part I of this book provided the counselor or caregiver with general information about dying and grieving and about the issues that may come up in working with dying patients and their families. Part II is designed to build skills that will directly aid in work with the dying and grieving client or patient.

Chapters Five and Six present information and exercises to aid in acquiring the attention, listening, and responding skills that a person needs in order to do this work. Attention skills, especially, are the foundation of any counseling work, and the process of learning to pay attention will also reveal to the counselor his own perceptions of death and how these perceptions may affect interactions with clients.

The material on attention and the exercises presented are based on the author's own training with Dr. Kathleen Speeth.[2] The listening and responding skills are based on Rogerian principles of psychotherapy.[3] The attention skills should be learned before the listening and responding skills, since there is a natural progression from paying attention and understanding silently to learning how to respond appropriately. Learning to listen and clearly respond is essential because the basic premise of this kind of work is that the client generally knows what is best for himself. When counseling the dying, emphasis must be placed on helping the client to understand how he can die an "appropriate" death and to give him support along the way.

Because people in the helping professions tend to give so much of themselves to others and because of the stressful nature of this work, Chapter Seven explores the experience of "burnout" and suggests some ways of preventing it. This chapter concludes with a discussion of "peak performance" as a possible lifestyle in which burnout would be unlikely to occur.

Chapter Eight deals with the counselor's own questions, feelings, concerns, and experiences with death and grief. The counselor or caregiver must understand his own relationship to death so that it will not interfere unconsciously with his interactions with the client. This chapter uses role-playing, discussions, and self-exploration exercises to probe the counselor's attitudes, concerns, beliefs, and experiences with death and grief.

Each chapter in this section presents some introductory information, followed by a group of exercises. These exercises have been selected for use by the reader alone or with one or two friends or colleagues. Larger group exercises and exercises that are difficult to complete in the absence of a skilled trainer have been omitted from this book, as have certain exercises (especially in the chapter on personal exploration of death and grief) believed to be too sensitive for many people to complete alone. The complete set of exercises is found in a companion volume to this book, *Working with the Dying and Grieving: A Trainer's Manual.*

BENEFITS OF HAVING A TRAINER

While the exercises in this book can be undertaken alone or in a small group without a trainer present, the training generally will be more effective when a skilled trainer is available. An experienced trainer will be able to help trainees become aware of their unconscious belief systems and prejudices, which may affect both their learning and their work with clients. For example, a counselor trained at Kara had lost her daughter in an accident a year and a half earlier, but felt she was "recovered" enough to begin counseling others. During the training it became evident that she was overidentifying with the client role and imposing her own ways of coping on the "client." The trainer was able to gently but firmly point out what she was doing and suggest ways in which she might avoid this problem in working with clients.

An experienced trainer also can provide more realism to the role-playing and other exercises that require some knowledge of the feelings and behaviors of dying and grieving clients. A trainer's instructions to the trainee may vary from a simple "Be a dependent client" to a detailed description of the client's history and situation. Trainees thus are able to experience situations similar to those they will encounter as counselors.

And finally, the trainer will be alert to signs that an exercise is too disturbing to be valuable for the trainee. There is always the potential for intimate and painful material to come up, and the availability of a skilled trainer to help structure and control the experience can be important at times.

INTRODUCTORY EXERCISES

Before turning to the attention skills in Chapter Five, complete one or more of the following introductory exercises. They are designed to start you thinking about the counseling role and the qualities and skills you may be bringing to it. At Kara exercises such as these also help to familiarize the trainer with the orientations of individual trainees.

Exercise: My Ideal Helper

Time: 10 minutes writing, unlimited discussion.

Adapted from: Dale Larson, Ph.D., *Mental Health Skills for Hospice Workers: Experiential Exercises.* Unpublished manuscript. Dale Larson, Division of Counseling Psychology, University of Santa Clara, Santa Clara, Ca. 95053.

Description:

1. Imagine and list on paper qualities you would like in a counselor. Focus on qualities that would support you in disclosing private and intimate thoughts and feelings.
2. Share with a friend or colleague if possible. Explore what qualities you have, and what you would like to learn more about.

Reasons for Using:

1. To define what skills are needed to do this work.
2. To identify skills you may choose to develop or incorporate into your work.

Materials:

Paper, pen.

Notes:

1. Draw on knowledge and experience you already have about helping relationships that work successfully.

Exercise: Myself as Helper, Real/Ideal

Time: 15-20 minutes

Adapted from: Dr. Gerald Goodman, SASHA tapes, © 1982, Reprinted by permission.*

Description:

1. With a friend or colleague, take turns playing the roles of Discloser and Listener.
2. The Discloser identifies something about himself that he thinks he needs to develop in order to be a supportive counselor (Example: [real] "I cut people off.").
3. Discloser then comes up with a solution to this or a way of improving. (Example: [ideal] "Be more patient.")
4. The Listener's task is to listen and help the Discloser to sharpen the contrast between the actual and the ideal, nothing more.
5. After 3-5 minutes, reverse roles and repeat.
6. Examine and discuss your interactions, pointing up Listener responses that were most helpful to the Discloser.

Reasons for Using:

1. To identify listening behaviors that help the Discloser with the problem.
2. To learn how to give feedback without imposing judgments.
3. To recognize one's natural counseling style.

Materials/Resources:

None.

Notes:

1. Sample considerations when discussing interactions:
   - Was advice given?
   - Did Listener attempt to solve the problem? (He should not.)
   - What kinds of questions were asked?
   - Which of Listener's responses were most helpful? (Be specific.)
   - What was said or done that did not help to clarify the real/ideal contrast?

- What do you want to increase or decrease in your helping interactions?
- Was there judging or condemning?

*SASHA tapes available from Dept. of Psychology, University of California, Los Angeles, Los Angeles, Ca. 90290 ($70) with 10 manuals for running groups.

Exercise: Questionnaire

Time: 1 hour—unlimited

Description:

1. Answer the questions below on another piece of paper.
2. Discuss your answers with a friend whom you trust, and explore what questions you want to pay attention to as you continue this book.

Reasons for Using:

1. To explore your current understanding of and experiences with death and grief.
2. To examine what areas you want to explore further.

Materials:

Paper and pen.
Questionnaire.

QUESTIONNAIRE

1. Give a brief description of your personal history with death, loss, or grief. What happened and what was your emotional response? Is there unfinished business?

2. Have you ever done psychological work on your relationship with death? If so, briefly describe it.

3. Have you ever talked about dying with your family? How do/did your parents relate to death or illness? What were you taught as a child?

4. Do you have a current philosophical/spiritual viewpoint about death? What is it and what factors drew you to this belief?

5. Is there anything specific that you want to focus on as you continue with this book?

6. Is there anything more you want to know about yourself and your relationship to death, grief, or loss?

7. Take a separate piece of paper and free associate, writing at least 60 words on the topic *MY DEATH*. Don't think before you write or worry about spelling, what is "right" to say, etc. Keep it to reflect on again after you complete this book or after 6 months of working with the dying and grieving.

REFERENCES

[1] H.J.M. Nouwen, *Out of Solitude,* Notre Dame, Ind.: Ave Maria Press, 1974, p. 40.

[2] K. Speeth, Ph.D., at the California Institute of Transpersonal Psychology, Menlo Park, California, 1978-1982.

[3] C. Rogers, *Client-Centered Therapy,* Boston, Mass.: Houghton-Mifflin, 1951.

CHAPTER FIVE

ATTENTION SKILLS

Attention skills should be specially emphasized when learning to work with the dying. The dying client, more than any other, may rely on nonverbal cues, and the counselor needs to pay close attention to these cues and to notice how his own emotional response affects what he observes. While most people unconsciously use attention skills, the training in attention presented here does not assume that the counselor has voluntary mastery of them. Based on Kathleen Speeth's work, this chapter provides a framework for learning the practice of *conscious* attention.[1]

Attention can be defined as a process of noticing, as impartially as possible, both internally and externally, whatever is happening at a given moment. Because judgment and expectations get in the way of noticing, paying attention involves a suspension of judgment and a willingness to encounter the unknown.

The act of paying attention also provides a sense of presence in the counseling situation, which Bugental describes as "being in a situation in which one intends to be as aware and as participative as one is able to be at that time and in those circumstances."[2] Accessibility and expressiveness, he says, are two basic qualities in "presence," the first arising from the intention to allow what happens to influence one, the second from the commitment to being open and to putting forth some effort.

Attention has been described in a similar manner in both the psychological and the spiritual literature, but it is primarily the religious practices that actually teach the skills of meditative attention. The psychiatrist T. Reik[3] distinguished between voluntary (focused) and involuntary (free-floating) attention by comparing them to a searchlight. Focused attention is turned toward a particular area in anticipation of something appearing. Free-floating attention scans the environment in a wide radius, lighting up one area after another.

Ordinary attention is focused in one direction only, but therapeutic attention can be divided between the self and the other (inside and outside) and at the same time it can be used to notice whether the focus is currently internal or external (See Figure 3.). This third focus of attention is called the "witness position," as it is used only to observe the direction of attention at a given moment.[4]

The counselor must learn to split his attention between internal and external events and between focused concentration and panoramic

FIGURE 3
ORDINARY AND THERAPEUTIC ATTENTION*

ordinary attention is in one direction

but attention can be divided between the outside and inside

and attention can be used to notice whether the
attention is outside or inside

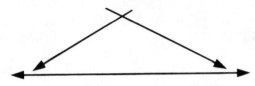

*Source: K. Speeth, "On Psychotherapeutic Attention," *Journal of Transpersonal Psychology,* p. 143, 14(2):141-160, 1982.

attention. He also needs to learn to notice where his attention is focused at any given time. Therapeutic attention consists of (a) the counselor's narrow focused immersion with the client, which is described as "matching"; (b) the counselor's focused attention on himself, which includes looking at one's own internal dialogue, boundaries, associations; and (c) the counselor's panoramic or free-floating attention that, without grasping or judging, notices what is happening with the client and what is happening within himself. Separate from these is the witness position, which simply observes where attention is focused and what quality it has. The witness position provides information on when, how, and where attention is being used.

This chapter defines these four aspects of attention in some detail. The first section describes focused attention on the client. It is followed by exercises that will teach you how to focus concentrated attention on another person. The second section explores the focusing of concentrated attention on the self. It is followed by another series of exercises that teach attention to the inner dialogue as well as looking at boundaries, limit setting, and focusing. While these two sections are described in sequence, the counselor ultimately needs to learn to experience inward and outward attention simultaneously. Simultaneous attention is achieved through the panoramic view, which is described next, along with a fuller explanation of the witness position. The chapter ends with a series of exercises that teach panoramic awareness and the witness position.

LEARNING ATTENTION SKILLS

The best way to learn the attention skills is to read about each aspect and apply it immediately by practicing its corresponding experiential exercises. The exercises themselves teach the skills more thoroughly than the didactic information. Problems that come up usually reflect (a) the trainee's frustration with not performing the skills "perfectly," (b) the tendency to judge oneself, or (c) fear or uncertainty about giving and receiving feedback. Therefore, it is important to understand that mastery of these skills takes much disciplined practice. This training provides the foundation and structure of the practice, which can then be continued throughout the counselor's career.

Often a counselor may get confused about what to do when he finds himself overwhelmed either by the client's material, his own material, or the process of trying to balance attention. To maintain balance, it is a good idea always to keep a piece of your attention focused on your own body. You can feel your foot on the floor, the teacup in your hand, or your buttocks on the chair.[5] This helps you remember yourself regardless of what is going on around you. This piece of attention will help you to maintain some objectivity in the face of a client's pain, sorrow, or fear.

The second problem is self-judgment. An essential part of the practice of being a counselor is the intention to maintain unconditional positive regard for oneself. You need to hold yourself in as much grace as you do your client. When learning new skills, one naturally feels awkward and insecure. Counselors often feel tongue-tied or inadequate and want to be reassured. "How can I dare think I have anything to offer anyone on this most intimate experience?" "I am so self-conscious; I can't think of anything to say."

It is common for counselors to try to deal with the content of the client's grief, forgetting that their presence and attention are the most important factors of all. Remember that the phase of self-doubt and awkwardness is natural in any learning process. These skills, which may at first seem difficult to learn, will become integrated into your normal way of being, just as do the skills involved in driving an automobile. Remember also that this feeling of vulnerability, of being out of control, is similar to that which clients are experiencing. Remembering the "taste" of this feeling can be important to a counselor in working with a client.

Another by-product of learning to be gentle with oneself is that you will model a behavior that the client can match. Matching goes two ways. The client will unconsciously match the counselor during a session, just as the counselor matches the client. If the counselor can hold himself and the client in a nest of unconditional positive regard, he can provide a presence that itself will heal. The counselor thus needs to practice being deeply centered, in order not only to meet the client with compassion but to provide a model for the client to match.

It is also important to remember the caution mentioned earlier about limits. Every counselor has the right not to pay attention to anything that he does not want to. Don't feel you have to talk about what does not feel right to you. The most important thing is to be genuine. Your ability to set limits results from your own positive self-regard. Being present means bringing all of who you are, including the limited or limiting parts, to the relationship and responding to what is happening in the moment.

Another problem counselors encounter is that of giving and receiving feedback. Feedback is an essential part of training in counseling skills. The counselor must learn how he is perceived in the counseling session, and he can learn this only through feedback. This means that at least some of the exercises must be undertaken with a partner, and that the partners must learn to give feedback in a constructive way. Most people have a natural desire to be liked and thus not to hurt or alienate others. Learning to give appropriate feedback and to accept and incorporate the constructive criticisms of others is an important part of a counselor's early training.

Feedback can be given effectively by using "I" statements that report personal responses to observable behavior. The most important part of giving feedback is differentiating between the observed behavior and one's personal reactions to it. It is important to avoid "you are" statements that make the other person feel rejected. Larson and Garfield describe effective feedback as: requested (implicitly if not overtly); timely (offered as soon as possible after the behavior); straightforward (simple language); concise and to the point; related to observed behavior rather than assumed motivations; helpful and non-judgmental; practical (focused on things a person can do something about); combining praise and constructive criticism; and discussed (to check that messages sent are those received).[6]

FOCUSED ATTENTION ON THE CLIENT

Empathy includes both identifying with the client and maintaining a sense of separation. Empathy can be described as the willingness to enter a relationship and respond truthfully to it. It involves the use of all the sensitivity that a counselor can elicit. It is a process of absorbing internally as much as the counselor can understand of the client's experience and reflecting this back to the client.

The process of empathy requires that you free yourself to see, understand, and experience life through another's being, to "sense" the client's inner world of private, personal meanings as if it were your own, but without ever losing the "as if" quality.[7]

This section focuses on sensing the client's inner world. When the counselor's attention is thus focused only on the client in the counseling relationship, identification or merging occurs. This is an essential part (but only a part) of appropriate counseling. This emptying of the self and confluence with the client has also been called "matching."[8] Matching actually is not a new skill. Very young children learn it in order to cope with their family situation. For example, a child may be so attuned to his mother that on entering the room he will know whether or not it is a good time to ask her for a favor. Matching requires sensitivity not only to another person's overt behavior, but also to other visual, auditory, and kinesthetic cues. These can include breathing and body posture, tone and speed of voice, skin color, and the physical distances between people.

Matching can be effectively used when the counselor consciously imitates (physically or in the imagination) and experiences personally these cues of the client. The client may display minute muscle changes (such as changes in the shape of the lower lip), subtle skin color changes, or a shift in breathing patterns when an emotional change has taken place. As the counselor pays attention to these cues, he needs to sense them in his own body. He should practice shifting back and forth between observing outside visible cues and noticing his own internal state, which will reflect his identification with the client as well as his own feelings.

Paying attention to the client is the first half of empathic counseling skills. The second half, disengagement and paying attention to the self, is described after the exercises on matching skills.

MATCHING EXERCISES

There is no talking in the counselor role during many of the attention exercises. This is in order to simplify and clarify the process of attention, to increase the counselor's awareness of other senses, and to eliminate talking as a natural antidote to anxiety. These exercises are not a rehearsal for everyday interactions. They model extreme behavior to teach the attention skills that can be incorporated into the everyday world.

Exercise: Matching an Emotion
(Practicing unconditional positive regard) from: K. Speeth, Ph.D.

Time: 30 minutes

Description:

1. Do this with a friend or colleague. Person A (client role) thinks about a real-life emotional situation of loss or grief. Do not talk. Shut your eyes if you want.
2. Person B (counselor role) empties the self out and silently matches the other, noting facial expression, breathing, posture, movement. He also notes his own internal experience. (Physically imitate posture and breathing if you want.)
3. After 5 minutes of matching, Person B tells Person A what he experienced through the matching (e.g., "At first I felt rapid breathing and anxiety; then it seemed to smooth out and I felt more peaceful.").
4. Person A confirms or corrects the observations. 10 minutes talking. Switch positions and repeat.

Reasons for Using:

1. Learning about matching and getting feedback on intuitions and empathy.
2. The goal is to discover how we pick up non-verbal cues, and to learn what is ours and what is the client's.

Materials:

None.

Notes:

1. This is an opportunity to begin to discriminate between the counselor's projected material and real observations of the client.
2. There may be anxiety about personal physical space and being watched. The person in the client role should feel free to take the needed space and to shut his eyes.

Exercise: Silent Matching
(Attention on the Client)

Time: 1½ hours

Description:

1. Do this with a partner. Person in client role talks for 10 minutes about an emotional issue of current significance in relationship to work with dying or grieving clients.
2. Person in counselor role matches client for entire time, without nodding, talking, or smiling. Pay attention to the client and match him.
3. Client/counselor share observations for 10 minutes, then switch roles and repeat steps 1 - 3.

Reasons for Using:

1. Practice in matching, and understanding the value of silent attention.

Materials:

Pencil and paper.

Notes:

1. This exercise teaches the value of a quiet, attentive presence. The silence becomes an ally and is less anxiety provoking.
2. It also will promote close connections between the participants as personal experience and feelings are shared.

Exercise: Visual Acuity Improvement

Time: 15 Minutes

Description:

1. Find a friend or colleague. Person A asks Person B five questions that he knows will be answered with a "Yes." Person B verbally answers the questions.
2. Person A then asks five questions that he knows will be answered with a "No."
   When asking these questions watch muscle tone, muscle changes in the face, posture, breathing, color in the face, shape of the lower lip.

3. Person A now asks five questions that he does not know the answer to. By watching the visual cues of Person B, Person A then guesses the response.
4. Switch roles and repeat steps 1 - 3.

Reasons for Using:

Practice in observing visual cues.

Materials:

None.

Notes;

Guessing the right answer is not as important as the experience of paying attention to visual cues.

Exercise: Observing Visual Cues

Time: ½ hour

Description:

1. Do this with a partner. Person A silently sits and thinks of an emotional event in his life, for 3 minutes. Person B observes visual cues and matches, watching breathing, coloring of face and hands, posture, muscle tone, and changes.
2. Person A tells Person B briefly about the event.
3. Person A then sits silently thinking of a second event with very different emotional components for 3 minutes. Person B matches.
4. Person A shares this event briefly.
5. Person A returns to one of these two events. Person B matches A, and decides which event Person A is considering.
6. Switch roles and repeat steps 1 - 6.

Reasons for Using:

To develop skills of observation and matching.

Materials:

None.

Notes:

This is a fairly easy exercise. The most important part is practicing the skill and developing the ability to observe and match.

Exercise: "Matching" Homework
from K. Speeth, Ph.D.

Time: Unlimited

Description:

1. Watch television with the sound off and practice matching the emotions. (Soap operas and dramas are suggested.) Turn the sound on now and again to check out your perceptions.
2. Consciously try to match your spouse, children, or colleagues throughout the week.

Notes:

This exercise can help you to recognize how much can be learned through observation.

FOCUSED ATTENTION ON THE SELF

Contact and Withdrawal
Other than observing the external clues displayed by the client, the primary source of understanding the counselor has is the observation of his own internal emotions, associations, and images. Some internal associations will be a direct result of matching the client; others will be the counselor's alone. The challenge is to differentiate between what is personal and what comes from understanding the client so that one can respond from understanding rather than projection. The counselor should recognize, as well, that he is capable of feeling his own version of what the client is describing.

Empathy involves matching the client but also maintaining a separate sense of self-awareness. There is real danger in total identification with the client, since losing the self to the client's emotions may lead to both of them becoming lost—a double drowning.

The grieving client needs his counselor to remain anchored in himself, thus freeing him to go deeply into his experience, knowing that the counselor will be there to bring him back to safety if necessary. "Thus therapists are doubly at risk: they stand a chance of losing a feeling of being securely grounded in their own being, and they are in danger of unknowingly bearing the heavy burdens of many others who are presumably less fortunate than they in terms of the sheer weight of suffering in their lives."[9]

A counselor therefore must learn how to disengage from as well as enter into identification with the client. This insures that he will remain a stable force that will be of some help to the client. To be in a position of voluntarily withdrawing identification, the counselor must be continually aware of his own boundaries and know and trust his own ability to separate from the client's emotional state. An intimate connection is based on the counselor's willingness to say "no" as well as "yes."[10]

Focusing

Kara counselors often ask what to do with the projections, observations, or associations that arise when they are working with dying or grieving clients. Usually it is appropriate merely to notice personal business during the session and put it aside to explore later. But there are no hard and fast rules for behavior with a client except to be true to the commitment of being fully present.

To aid in this, E. Gendlin developed a process called "focusing," which can be used by the counselor to explore the feelings that arise internally after meeting with a client.[11] Focusing is useful when a person feels "out of sorts" from working with a client. It can help in clarifying underlying emotions and is an excellent way to practice the general technique of paying attention to the self and regarding whatever comes up with an attitude of acceptance. Focusing involves asking oneself "How do I feel right now?" and sitting back for the response. The technique is most useful, after seeing a client, when the counselor realizes some personal feelings have been rekindled through the process of paying attention.

The techniques of focusing are briefly outlined below. There are several fine books describing it in more detail. [12]

1. First get comfortable. Some kind of relaxation exercise may help.

2. Find your "felt sense" by asking yourself how you feel or by remembering the difficult situation or current problem.

3. Form a mental image of the situation or find some words to describe your feelings. Then look inside. Where is that feeling located? It is not usually specifically located in a tense muscle but is more a vague subtle thickening of feeling inside.

4. Next put a label on that feeling in the body. Try new words until you find the one that describes it exactly. (Do not think about the situation, but focus on the bodily sensation of it and describe that.)

The felt sense is not always there all at once when you turn your attention inward. It's as though all of the feeling information was spread thinly throughout your body until you stop and take the time to let a felt sense form. Then, during that quiet moment, the information that is spread out moves towards the center, as though it were being attracted by a magnet, and into the "felt sense," which becomes clearer and stronger as you wait quietly.[13]

5. Now go back and forth between the words, the image, and the feeling in the body until a "shift" occurs. This felt shift is the goal of focusing. It should be some form of tension release and should produce a sense of clarity.

The felt shift, or tension release, may be an "aha!" experience or a small and subtle shift in perception. Either way, something has changed, and the problem or feeling will seem different. These steps can be practiced alone or with a partner. But first try the following exercises on developing awareness of self.

Exercise: Awareness of Self
(Focused Attention on the Self)

Time: Unlimited

Description:

Sit quietly and pay attention to any physical sensations in your body, anything you feel. Do not try to change the sensations, but notice where you are relaxed or are tense. What areas have no feeling at all? As you pay attention, do any new sensations arise?

Reasons for Using:

To provide a structure for the practice of self-awareness.

Materials:

None

Notes:

This exercise is particularly good for people with no experience in meditating. It can be a first step in learning to pay attention to the self.

Exercise: Attention on One's Self
  (Vipassana Attention to Self)

Time: 20 minutes

Description:

1. Find a private spot and talk out loud about whatever comes to mind for 5-10 minutes.
2. Say whatever comes up, even if there is resistance.
3. Write down or discuss with a partner:
   a. Resistance to, or acceptance of, the exercise.
   b. Personal reactions to the process of following the mind.
   c. Relationship of exercise with meditation practice.

Reasons for Using:

To observe your own mind and emotions.

Materials:

None

Notes:

You may be self-conscious about talking out loud, especially if others are in the room. It is a good idea to talk about resistances to doing this exercise. Books on meditation are included in the bibliography.

Exercise: Developing Intuition
  from: Frances Vaughan, Ph.D., *Awakening Intuition,* p. 59, New York: Anchor Books, 1979.

Time: Unlimited

Description:

Keep a journal of hunches, flashes of insight, or presentiments you experience. Write the hunch down, be it negative, positive, or neutral. Then you can check to see if any of these were correct and can learn to separate imagination, anxiety, and real intuition. Only through awareness and practice can you learn about this.

Materials:

Journal

Notes:

Don't worry about being right or wrong. Errors also teach you about conscious mind and personal interests. This works best if you meet with others periodically to discuss and support each other in your development.

PANORAMIC ATTENTION AND THE WITNESS POSITION

Choiceless Awareness or Panoramic Attention

Panoramic attention is awareness invested evenly in all things, associated with ". . . a feeling of impartiality, of spaciousness, of breadth of vision."[14] This form of attention allows the therapist to freely notice whatever is occurring without censorship, both internally and externally, avoiding identification with either the client or himself.

The counselor can best serve the client by being willing to be surprised each time they meet. Judgment is suspended when the counselor's attention is panoramic. If the counselor is concerned about his own performance or has any fixed expectations about the client or their relationship, he will not be using free-floating or panoramic attention. Panoramic attention requires a meditative practice of nonjudgmental awareness.

The Witness Position

The witness position is similar in style to maintaining panoramic awareness. The witness is that part of the counselor's attention that is reserved for watching the process itself. It is impartial, nonjudgmental, and evenly hovering.

> While allowing most of the attention to play freely upon what the client is saying and doing, and what associations I have to it, how interested I am and how empathetic, I reserve just a little attention to notice all this flux. I allow my attention to play freely or to zoom into deep identification, yet I sustain a bit of myself above it. When I am immersed I watch my almost total immersion; when I am engaged in evenly hovering attention I watch that.[15]

Practicing the witness position will teach you where your focus of attention is and thus help you to develop the ability to move voluntarily from one focus to another.

The exercises that follow teach panoramic awareness and witness consciousness using both Freud's free association technique and the traditional Gestalt awareness exercise developed by Fritz Perls.[16] In subsequent chapters, where three people are involved in an exercise, the observer's role is to practice the witness position.

Exercise: Free Association
(Panoramic or Evenly Hovering Attention)

Time: 1½ hrs.

Description:

1. Do this with a partner.
2. Person A (client) talks for ½ hour with eyes closed, following whatever comes to mind. If material is too private, just say "censor."
3. Person B (counselor) practices evenly-hovering attention silently, while the client practices following his own mind.
4. Share experiences for 15 minutes.
5. Switch positions and repeat.

Reasons for Using:

To teach both paying attention to the self (client's free association) and paying panoramic attention (counselor position).

Notes:

The counselor practices listening to the client with attention balanced equally between himself and the other. This exercise provides an excellent opportunity to practice the witness position as well. This often is a very powerful exercise. Give yourself time after it to talk to each other about it.

Exercise: Continuum of Awareness
(Panoramic or Evenly-Hovering Attention) from: Perls, Hefferline & Goodman, *Gestalt Therapy,* p. 82, New York: Crown Books, 1951.

Time: 45 minutes

Description:

1. Do this with a partner.
2. Person A (counselor) becomes a still, silent presence paying attention to Person B (client), matching him and watching himself.
3. Person B:

    "(1) Maintain the sense of actuality—the sense that your awareness exists now and here. (2) Try to realize that *you* are living the experience; acting it, observing it, suffering it, resisting it. (3) Attend to and follow up all experiences, the "internal" as well as the "external," the abstract as well as the concrete, those that tend toward the past as well as those that tend toward the future, those that you "wish," those that you "ought," those that simply "are," spontaneously. (4) With regard to every experience without exception, verbalize: "Now I am aware that . . ."[17] Repeat this over and over for a 10 minute period. Report what you are aware of.
4. Switch positions and repeat.

Reasons for Using:

To practice panoramic attention.

Materials:

None.

Notes:

This is a basic Gestalt exercise. It teaches the process of moving attention, and seeing the self as separate rather than one with the client (as in matching). It also is a good exercise for putting the counselor in the present awareness of what is going on, which is one of the goals of counseling (as well as a goal when working on death). This exercise is sometimes unpleasant or anxiety provoking and difficult to do correctly. Ten minutes may be too short to overcome self-consciousness and recognize the benefits of the exercise. If so, extend the time limit.

Exercise: Evenly-Hovering Attention
adapted from: K. Speeth, Ph.D.

Time: 1 hour

Description:

1. Ask two friends to have a conversation about something emotional that will engage them.
2. Sit next to your two friends with a piece of paper in front of you that has the following form:

When _____ said	I experienced

3. When one of your friends says or does something that you respond to in any way, write down his or her statement and your feeling response. For example:

When Sue said	I remembered
that she loved her brother	my brother as a little boy and felt love for him

Reasons for Using:

This is the culminating exercise combining attention to the other with attention to the self and watching both sides from an unattached witness position.

Materials:

Pen and paper.

Notes:

You do not need to share your responses with your friends. That way you can avoid censoring. This is a difficult exercise and usually requires much practice before you become proficient at separating their words from your feelings. It is well worth the time and effort; it is an excellent way to develop a sense of your boundaries and projections and to practice the witness position.

REFERENCES

[1]K. Speeth, "On Psychotherapeutic Attention." *Journal of Transpersonal Psychology,* 14(2):141-160, 1982.

[2]J. Bugental, *Psychotherapy and Process,* Menlo Park, Calif.: Addison-Wesley, 1978, p. 37.

[3]T. Reik, *Listening with the Third Ear,* New York: Farrer, Strauss, 1948.

[4]*Supra* note 1, p. 143.

[5]*Ibid.,*

[6]D. Larson, and C. Garfield, *Berkeley Hospice Training Manual,* Berkeley, Calif.: Berkeley Hospice Training Project, 1982.

[7]C. Rogers, *Client Centered Therapy,* Boston: Houghton Mifflin, 1951, p. 89.

[8]K. Speeth, lectures at California Institute of Transpersonal Psychology, Menlo Park, Calif. 1978-1980.

[9]*Supra* note 1, p. 150.

[10]S. Luthman, *Intimacy: the Essence of Male and Female,* San Rafael, Calif.: Mehetabel, 1982.

[11]E. Gendlin, *Focusing,* New York: Bantam Books, 1981.

[12]*Ibid.*, Kathleen McGuire Boukydis, *Building Supportive Community: Mutual Self-Help Through Peer Counseling,* 186 Hampshire St., Cambridge, Mass.: Center for Supportive Community, 1981; D. Larson and C. Garfield, *Berkeley Hospice Training Manual,* Berkeley, Calif.: Berkeley Hospice Training Project, 1982.

[13]Boukydis, *ibid.,* p. 111.

[14]*Supra* note 1, p. 151.

[15]*Ibid.,* p. 155.

[16]F. Perls, R. Hefferline, and P. Goodman, *Gestalt Therapy,* New York: Dell, 1951.

[17]*Ibid.,* p. 82.

CHAPTER SIX

LISTENING AND RESPONDING SKILLS

THE EMPATHIC RESPONSE[1]

The role of the listener is to help the discloser to understand his own experience. Listening is especially important when working with the dying or grieving. Often listening is all that one can do.

A Kara counselor recently met with Gina, whose twenty-three year old daughter had just died of a drug overdose. Gina was deeply grieving. She felt guilty, angry, and confused, and was overwhelmed by her emotions. The day after her daughter's funeral, Gina was so distraught that all the counselor could do was listen to her and empathize with her pain. The counselor later worried that she might not have done enough, but she came to understand that allowing Gina to express her feelings without interruption was something no one else had offered.

The first listening skill—attention—has already been described. The nonverbal communication of attention creates trust and a feeling of being understood. Eye contact and physical distance are also powerful communicators. Each culture has a different norm for these. In middle-class America, eye contact usually indicates interest and a willingness to communicate. However, the counselor should watch to see if direct eye contact is making the client uncomfortable. The counselor's posture is another nonverbal way of communicating. An open stance that is relaxed will provide a model for the client to match. The counselor should use natural gestures that communicate what he intends.

The counselor may find himself talking to the client when he could be just listening and making himself accessible. The average time between a person's remark and his companion's response is three-quarters of a second. When practicing counseling skills, it is a good idea for the counselor to allow for a longer response time in order to get into the habit of being more comfortable with the silent spaces between the words.

Often a counselor's verbal responses come from his sense of helplessness or some level of intolerance for the pain of facing the unalterable course of dying or grief. The unconscious urge to try to "fix" the situation is common for newly trained counselors. This is not to say that one should not respond to the client's practical needs. But there is a difference between acting to support the client and attempting to solve an unsolvable problem.

Empathic listening and responding is based on the concept that the client knows best how to heal himself. This means that the best a counselor can do sometimes is to reflect back what he thinks he heard or understood. A major goal of active listening is to help the client connect words and feelings. The assumption is that if one truly experiences a feeling, a shift occurs. Putting a label on a feeling creates structure, a sense of control, and an opportunity to experience it fully. To experience a feeling one must first find it, define it, and acknowledge it. The counselor can aid this process by reflecting feelings; paraphrasing; asking open-ended or specific questions; inviting the client to focus on feelings and to define and clarify them; summarizing, and sharing personal responses, including feedback.[2] These six response styles will now be explored in more detail.

Reflection of feelings. This involves paying attention to more than the words that are spoken, looking at nonverbal cues and checking inside yourself to see what feelings you are matching. In response to these cues, you can verbally check out your perceptions on the feeling level. The client may either agree with or contradict you. Either way, the interaction will help the client to clarify and focus, and you will learn more about the client and yourself.

Paraphrasing. This involves the same process, but larger portions of the communication are reflected back. The position of the listener allows you to watch for connecting threads of emotion or thought from a more objective position than the client's. The client may find himself focusing more and more inwardly as he gets more deeply involved. It will help him feel less isolated if he knows that someone is watching over the whole picture and helping to clarify.

The counselor should reflect feelings using the same language as the client. This involves auditory, visual, or kinesthetic expressions. For example, if the client talks in visual terms, using the words "see" and "looks like," the counselor should also use visual language. That in itself gives the client the impression of being understood.

In addition, the counselor should reflect with words of the same intensity. If the client is only mildly frustrated, the observation "You're really enraged" would be inappropriate unless the counselor is picking up nonverbal cues. An exercise at the end of the chapter will help you to identify feelings.

Asking open and closed questions. Open questions elicit more than a "yes" or "no" response, and they tend to lead a person deeper into his feelings and thoughts. Examples of open questions are: "Would you tell me more about that?" "What does this mean to you?" or "How does that feel?" Open questions ask for clarification and elaboration. A client may say one word that seems to represent all his feelings. The counselor could then ask the client to return to that word and perhaps say more about it. Closed questions elicit a "yes" or "no" response, such as, "Is the pain bad today?" An open version of that question would be, "Tell me what your pain is like today" or "I'm wondering what your pain feels like."

Open questions are generally more effective than closed questions, but the counselor should make use of both types. Questions, however, should not exceed 20 percent of the conversation; if they do, the conversation is revolving around the counselor's frame of reference instead of the client's.[3]

Definition and clarification. In this as in previous techniques, the counselor is inviting the client to focus on feelings. What is added here is to encourage the client to explore these feelings more directly, to acknowledge a feeling and take responsibility for it. The counselor can help the client to use the focusing technique or to pay attention to body sensations, if it seems appropriate. It is important for the counselor to allow time for a feeling to be expressed and then to acknowledge it. Acknowledgement often occurs at a nonverbal level, as when the counselor feels his own eyes fill when a client is very sad. Matching communicates caring. When a client and a counselor share a moment of genuine understanding, there is often a release of tension and a feeling of warmth in the acknowledgement that contact has been made.

Summarization. This is a useful way to conclude a session. It helps to clarify that the counselor understands what has been said, gives the client an opportunity to correct the counselor's understanding if necessary, and helps the counselor to clarify his own understanding of what has happened. It is also useful for shifting topics. Basically it indicates closure and a change in the interaction.

Sharing Personal Responses. A grieving person may need to hear about the counselor's personal experiences in order to feel safe. Personal sharing is often appropriate when counseling the dying and grieving, since the client may feel powerless and alone if the counselor only mirrors his feelings. Of course, a client may be asking the counselor about himself in order to avoid self-disclosure, or simply from social discomfort or habit. Boukydis offers some guidelines for balancing the interaction:

- Return to reflecting the client's feelings immediately after every self-disclosure.
- Reflect feelings three times more than any other response.[4]

Boukydis further describes five types of personal sharing that can be mixed in with reflections of feelings and open questions:

- Throw out a guess or intuition and describe it as such when reflecting feelings;
- Give feedback on perceptions of the client's behavior, posture, gestures, reflecting strengths and weaknesses in the client's behavior patterns as observed;
- Give more general negative or positive feedback (this feedback should be given with great care, since it is easily misinterpreted as rejection);
- Relate personal experiences (but do not downplay the importance of the client's experience);
- Give suggestions, advice, opinions (this too is risky since one rarely knows what is best for another person).[5]

Following are exercises for learning NonVerbal Attending Skills and Responding Skills presenting a variety of sophistication and intensity levels.

Exercise: Vignettes

Time: Unlimited

Description:

Vignettes are designed to be used with three participants doing roleplays. Following are a number of vignettes that can be assigned to counselor or client roles for roleplays. These have come from client situations, and were chosen for their provocative nature. Use them for practicing counseling skills. When roleplaying there should be a client, a counselor, and a witness role (see Notes below).

Reasons for Using:

Use these vignettes when it is inappropriate for those in the client role to talk about their own losses, or when a variety of specific case situations are needed to give the counselor role a chance to work with a specific feeling state.

Materials:

List of the roleplays.

Notes:

The client role, counselor role, and witness role model the three parts of each individual described in the chapter on attention skills: the part paying attention to the client, the part paying attention to the counselor, and the part which is the witness watching the whole process and putting it all together. The witness position is that of the observer who gives feedback. Some of the most valuable training occurs in this position. The witness develops the ability to move silently back and forth between external and internal observation. The person in the role of counselor faces the challenge of communicating and practicing reflecting skills. The client role provides the material to explore.

SAMPLE ROLEPLAYS

1. *Client:* You have just been told your cancer is terminal.

2. *Client:* You are angry at your doctor. You have cancer and do not know who to believe about how to cure it.

3. *Client:* You asked for a Kara counselor but are embarrassed. You can't be straight about wanting to see a counselor or not, nor about your embarrassment. (You are in pain over your spouse's death.)

4. *Client:* You are angry at your brother about his neglect of your dying mother. You give a long, boring monologue about the past sins of your brother.

5. *Client:* Present a confusing array of feelings about your terminal malignancy. You are angry, sad, fearful, hopeful, in pain, feel abandoned by friends, and long for death as an end to pain.

6. *Client:* Be "inaccessible," "depressed," "angry," or "dependent," and make up the content of the roleplay.

7. *Client:* You have just discovered that your spouse (who has been in the strong role in the relationship) is terminally ill and is rapidly becoming an invalid.

8. *Client:* You haven't felt right since the death of a business associate a month ago. By open questions you discover that the death of a brother five years earlier was left unresolved.

9. *Client:* You haven't felt right since your diagnosis of a fatal cancer, even though the symptoms are not yet apparent. You claim to have no fear of death because of strong religious convictions about the afterlife, but underneath this you feel sad, fearful, and angry.

10. *Client:* You are confused, angry, feeling abandoned following the death of your spouse. But you also feel guilty about feeling these emotions.

11. *Client:* You claim that you haven't been sleeping or eating well since your mastectomy one year ago. By open questions you discover that you have never dealt with the possibility of a fatal recurrence of your cancer, or your fear of death in general.

12. *Client:* This is three years following the death of your spouse (who left you well provided for). You are still unable to leave the house very often. You were referred to Kara by your minister who was concerned about your isolation. You profess no problems, but in fact are scared to deal with the world and your spouse's death.

13. *Counselor:* Your client's husband was seriously hurt in an accident at work. He was on the critical list, and you were not sure he would live. Five days ago the doctors said he would recover and go home in four days. The night before he was to go home, he died suddenly of a blood clot. You are devastated by the roller-coaster ride of hope and despair that you have just experienced.

14. *Client:* You have one eight-year-old daughter and a five-month-old son. Two years ago you had a stillborn daughter. Because of this you joined Compassionate Friends (national support group for parents who have lost children). One day a member was talking to you about the loss of her child through sudden infant death syndrome. The next morning when you were packing your daughter's school lunch, you heard your son crying. You left him for a bit, focusing on breakfast chores. Ten minutes later you went to his crib and found him still and not breathing. You gave him resuscitation, but he did not revive. The diagnosis was sudden infant death syndrome. You call a counselor one week later and talk about your guilt, anger, and confusion.

15. *Client:* You are a young resident on the oncology ward who was taking care of a young dental student with advanced cancer. You reported that your patient tried to engage you in conversation each morning on rounds. The patient would express concern about his condition; you would tell him not to worry and leave the room. You felt uncomfortable about this, realizing that the patient might benefit from talking with you, if only for a few minutes. When your thoughts were explored further, it occurred to you that what you feared was that the patient might express his sadness about not being able to finish dental school, or about not being able to get married as he had planned. When asked how you would feel if your patient began to cry, you replied that you were afraid that you would break down yourself. You then said that if the patient expressed his feelings it would make you aware that this could happen to you, and that you did not want to let such thoughts ever cross your mind. You want to talk about this with a counselor.

16. *Counselor:* Your client is a friendly, attractive eighteen-year-old woman with Hodgkin's disease. She has been undergoing chemotherapy for eight months. Two months ago she reported to the oncology clinic for her regularly scheduled visit. She had been very reliable about her previous clinic visits and on this visit she pleaded with the oncology fellow and nurse to postpone her chemotherapy as she did not want to be ill at her senior prom that evening. After some discussion, the decision was made to postpone chemotherapy for one week, at which time the patient did report to the clinic but was 1½ hours late. Three weeks later the patient failed to appear for her scheduled clinic visit. When contacted at home, she stated that she had decided she was well, and that she would return to the clinic if she felt ill. The client told you about all this. What will you say to her?

17. *Counselor:* You have been seeing a client for three or four visits and you are feeling uneasy. The initial reason given for contacting Kara was that the client had unresolved grief over the death of her husband six months ago. It is becoming increasingly clear to you that this person is really looking for a friend in her lonely world and is unwilling (or perhaps not needing) to discuss her grief over the loss of her husband.

18. *Counselor with counselor (on feedback):* You are uncomfortable because a fellow counselor is using degrading,

uncomplimentary terms to describe a client. She says the client is "a demanding bitch" ... "a real pain in the ass" ... "impossible."

19. *Counselor:* You're seeing a client who is describing sadness over a child's death but whose facial expression is smiling and there seems to be inappropriate laughter.

20. *Counselor, a family case:* The mother is dying of a paralyzing disease. She has an artificial voice box, but cannot move her body at all. She has two children. The youngest girl, age nine, is suddenly bedwetting at night and hoarding food at school. You came to see the children and the mother.

21. *Counselor:* A client calls whose mother killed herself a month earlier by stepping in front of a train. The client is not overly upset about the incident, and is considering applying to be a counselor. How do you ascertain her emotional situation? How can you serve her best?

22. *Counselor:* You arrive at the nursing home for the first visit with your client who is dying of lung cancer, brain cancer, and cirrhosis of the liver. She is alert, sitting up in bed and smoking a cigarette. Her left side is paralyzed. She hates the nursing home and is angry at the loss of her independence. She has had meatloaf five nights in a row. Fifteen minutes into your visit she is still very angry and asks you to leave. What do you do?

23. *Counselor:* You arrive for an appointment at your client's home to find him engrossed in a TV program. The telephone call from your client setting up this appointment suggested urgency and you made special arrangements so you could come today. The client doesn't offer to turn off the TV. What do you do?

24. *Counselor with counselor:* In small group, a counselor presents difficulties he is having with his client. You ask the counselor some questions to distinguish the heart of the problem. The counselor does not appear to hear you. He looks to the leader for an answer. You ask another question of the counselor. In answering he looks at the leader for verification, not at you. You feel angry at not being listened to or heard. What do you do?

25. *Counselor:* Your client is twice divorced, mother of a ten-year-old boy, and an active member of AA. She recently lost her father

to cancer and her relationship with her boyfriend is breaking up. As you are wrapping up a session, she looks sweetly at you, tells you what a help she thinks you have been for her, and asks you if you have had any close member of your family die? What and how much do you tell her?

26. *Counselor:* Your client's husband died suddenly from choking six months ago. In the first few meetings the client was open with her grief, crying and talking about her husband. At the end of three months of meetings with you, she refers to him occasionally. She has not gotten around to clearing out his closet. You are feeling bored in the sessions and not sure how to deal with her passivity.

27. *Counselor:* Every week for the last four months you arrive to find your client smiling and making tea for you. She talks mainly about her husband and his improvement from brain surgery. She has lupus, is on cortisone, and has stated that she knows that she would feel better if she lost forty pounds. She has let her nursing license expire and does not leave the house. She keeps telling you that when her husband is better she will do some of these things. Her husband can now be left alone. The client has made no attempt to do something for herself. You feel frustrated and are finding it hard to be supportive.

28. *Counselor:* You assess that it is time to end your sessions with your client. You have shared intimate and profound times together. You have a mutual love and appreciation. The client asks you to continue with her "as a friend" after the counseling relationship has ended. You do not want this, but do not want to hurt or abandon her.

Exercise: Listening Positions I

from: Dale Larson, Ph.D., *Mental Health Skills for Hospice Workers: Experiential Exercises.* Unpublished manuscript. Dale Larson, Div. of Counseling Psychology, University of Santa Clara, CA 95053.

Time: 15 minutes

Description:

1. Do this with a partner. Person A sits on the floor, Person B stands up.
2. Carry on a conversation from this position about any topic (use vignettes if you like).
3. Discuss how each feels.
4. Reverse positions and repeat.

Reasons for Using:

Critically ill clients are usually in bed. This gives counselors a sense of how the client may feel and the appropriate position to sit in.

Materials:

None.

Notes:

This is a basic exercise for beginners or for a break between more emotional exercises.

Exercise: The Listening Exchange II

In this, and the next two exercises, the listening skills have been separated into different skills to be practiced. Each successive exercise in this group provides more complexity and has a slightly different focus in basic skill building. It is difficult to do such fine differentiating and it may create self-consciousness. Eventually the skills will be incorporated into your natural style, and you will use them without thinking.

Time: 45 minutes approximately

Description:

1. Do this with two other people. Each person becomes a client, counselor, or observer/witness.
2. Client speaks about a current issue, a past loss, or uses a vignette role (speak in present tense for 10 minutes). Counselor *reflects feelings* and *asks open questions* (use postural, breath, and emotional matching). Observer/Witness observes self and interactions.

154

3. Allow feedback time. Client and counselor each say how it felt to them. Observer reports observations, using feedback guidelines (refer to Chapter 5).

Reasons for Using:

Basic skill building.

Materials:

None.

Notes:

Total time is at least 45 minutes, but usually the feedback lasts longer than 5 minutes.

In this exercise you are learning about three aspects of counseling:

1. The content of the client's material, especially if death-related, may bring up personal issues. Counselor and witness will learn about paying attention to self and other.
2. Reflective and questioning skills.
3. The feedback process.

Exercise: The Listening Exchange III

Time: 45 minutes

Description:

1. Do this with two other people. Each person becomes client, counselor, or observer/witness.
2. Client speaks about a current issue, or a past loss, or a vignette role (speak in present tense) for 10 minutes. Counselor *reflects feelings* and *asks open questions* (use postural, breath and emotional matching), and *paraphrases*. Observer/Witness observes self and interactions.
3. Allow feedback time: Client and counselor say how it felt to them; observer reports observations using feedback guidelines (in Chapter 5).
4. In this exercise, Counselor practices nonverbal responses, reflection of feelings, open questions, and paraphrasing.

Reasons for Using:

Basic skill building.

Materials:

None.

Notes:

Most participants match too well and forget themselves. As a result they often feel drained. Also, the strain of learning takes its toll. It is often helpful to intersperse roleplays with breaks, body stretches, and lighter material. It is very important to remember your boundaries and practice disengaging during the process, as well. You can do this by paying attention to a part of your body such as your foot or your back against the chair as you listen to your client.

Exercise: The Listening Exchange IV

Time: 45 minutes

Description:

1. Do this with two other people. Each person becomes client, counselor, or observer/witness.
2. Client speaks about a current issue, or a past loss, or a vignette role (speak in present tense) for 10 minutes. Counselor *reflects feelings* and asks *open questions* (use postural, breath and emotional matching), *focuses, shares personal feelings,* and *summarizes.* Observer/Witness observes self and interactions.
3. Allow feedback time: Client and counselor say how it felt to them; observer reports observations using feedback guidelines (in Chapter 5).
4. In this exercise, Counselor practices personal sharing, focusing, and summarization.

Reasons for Using:

Basic skill building.

Materials:

None.

Notes:

You may choose, during one round of this exercise, to forget what you have learned about listening and responding and see what comes up naturally. This can be an opportunity to see what difficulties arise.

Exercise: Listening Exchange V

Time: 2 to 2½ hours

Description:

1. Do this with two other people.
2. During the session, each person has a ½ hour turn as a *client, counselor,* and *observer/witness. Client* uses a vignette role, *counselor* uses *all* the listening and reporting skills. *Observer/Witness* watches and uses feedback guidelines when giving feedback in the end.
3. After each ½ hour exercise, each person writes notes about how he experienced his role. Then discuss the experiences.
4. Switch roles.

Reasons for Using:

Basic skill building.

Materials:

None.

Notes:

Take turns keeping time and moderating the feedback discussion. Timer should give *client/counselor* a two-minute reminder before end of turn. It will be tempting to get sidetracked if the client talks about intense feelings. It is important to be sensitive and equally important to move on when the time is up. The client can use a vignette, talk about a personal situation, or use the focusing techiques and talk about whatever comes up.

REFERENCES

[1]The discussion of listening and responding skills draws from the

author's own work, as well as from that of the following authors: K.M. Boukydis, *Building Supportive Community: Mutual Self-Help Through Peer Counseling,* 186 Hampshire St., Cambridge, Mass.: Center for Supportive Community, 1981; L. Brammer, *The Helping Relationship,* Englewood Cliffs, N.J.: Prentice-Hall, 1979, J. Bugental, *Psychotherapy and Process,* Menlo Park, Calif.: Addison-Wesley, 1978; C. Rogers, *Client-Centered Therapy,* Boston: Houghton-Mifflin, 1951.

[2]Boukydis, *supra* note 1.

[3]D. Larson and C. Garfield, *Berkeley Hospice Training Manual,* Berkeley, Calif.: Berkeley Hospice Training Project, 1982.

[4]Boukydis, *supra* note 1.

[5]*Ibid.*

CHAPTER SEVEN

AVOIDING BURNOUT

The helping professions are often structured to encourage "burnout," rather than support the counselor in maintaining the distance and self-control that can prevent it. Burnout occurs when one becomes exhausted by excessive personal demands on energy and resources. A person experiences many levels of stress before experiencing burnout, and all of these stages are reversible without having to quit one's job. When a person is truly "burned out" something is gone that does not return.[1]

People who work with dying patients often unconsciously match the emotions of their patients, experiencing anger, depression, denial, fear, and vulnerability. Both staff and patients feel anger and depression in reaction to helplessness and loss of control, though anger also can serve to reduce feelings of impotence. It is essential for people who work with the dying to have an outlet for their own emotions so they can continue the work without having to go numb.

The basic idea is to handle stress so that the stage of *burnout* is never reached. One way to do this is illustrated by the "peak performer," who takes an active, positive stance toward life and work. There is no trapped feeling for peak performers, no sense of being victimized.[2] Burnout is unlikely to occur because stress reduction is built into one's lifestyle.

Two primary sources of stress in any stress-filled job are the powerlessness or helplessness the worker individually may feel and the structure of the job or the organization itself. There are a number of ways both the individual and the organization can reduce stress, and in so doing reduce the likelihood of burnout. First let's look at some of the more common causes and signs of burnout in the work setting.[3]

CAUSES OF BURNOUT IN THE ORGANIZATION

- Lack of clear direction in the job role.
- Lack of organizational support for saying "no."
- Uncertainty of rewards.
- Lack of system within the organization for feedback to higher-ups.
- Lack of job security.
- No in-house support for emotions and for decision-making.

- Understaffing leading to overworking; too many clients or patients.
- Poor working conditions (disorganization, noise, clutter).
- Dehumanization of work; little opportunity for in-depth "people" contact.
- No built-in, spontaneous, voluntary "time-outs."

SIGNS OF IMPENDING BURNOUT IN THE INDIVIDUAL

- Hating work and clients.
- Making derogatory remarks or joking about clients.
- Compartmentalizing work and home.
- Intellectualizing and analyzing the situation instead of feeling emotional responses.
- Separating self from "them."
- Spending less time with patients or clients; minimizing contact with them.
- Somatic pains.
- Reduced productivity.
- Poor relations with other staff or clients.
- Insomnia.
- Going by the rules rather than seeing each situation as new.

WAYS TO PREVENT BURNOUT: THE ORGANIZATION

There are many ways a human service or health care organization can change the work environment to prevent burnout. Following are a few suggestions.

1. Vary work responsibilities so there are times of greater and lesser intensity.
2. Make organizational plans with clear objectives and realistic use of staff.
3. Provide yearly evaluations of the organization as well as of staff. Provide a clear outlet for feedback.
4. Provide rewards for workers, including non-monetary forms of recognition such as sabbaticals, retirement policies, educational opportunities, and in-service training.
5. Provide an environment that acknowledges the need for balance between internal and external pressures (e.g., by providing a "time-out" room or quiet corner).
6. Provide staff retreats that offer a change of pace. These could be educational, work-oriented, or simply recreational.

7. Recognize the importance of internal as well as external needs. Encourage support groups where staff can talk about feelings about the job and how it relates to their lives. Provide a time to discuss problems at work and a time for support for strong emotional responses to client situations. Trouble-shoot communication difficulties.

8. Give special training in interpersonal skills and personal stress reduction. Look at staff motivation for doing the work and their expectations of themselves and the organization.

9. Provide time to have fun without guilt.

WAYS TO PREVENT BURNOUT: THE INDIVIDUAL

1. Do some regular exercise that you enjoy (not that you "should" do), or use regular stress-reduction relaxation techniques. Eat well and reduce sugar intake.

2. Look at your life goals and develop an understanding of how your work relates to them. Make six-month, one-year, five-year, ten-year plans.

3. If there is no support group at work, find one outside your job.

4. Enjoy life, and do not sacrifice everything for your work. Create a lifestyle which fulfills you, so you do not need your client's love or attention.

5. Build in "time outs" so that you vary the intensity levels of your work.

6. Look at your life mission, assess it and note how it fits in with your work. Spend time alone, questioning, sharing, reading about values and purpose.

7. When counseling a client, reserve a part of yourself to witness the interaction. Focus a part of your attention on a part of your body to insure some separation from the client.

8. Try to define your personal boundaries and those of your clients or patients.

9. Develop a kindly attitude towards yourself. Develop the capacity to forgive yourself over and over again, and to suspend self-judgment.

10. Give yourself pleasure. When a counselor loves himself, his client will match that inner relationship as well.

11. Practice yelling "STOP" internally when you find yourself attacking yourself. Try to just drop the attack without giving it further attention.

VALUE OF A SUPPORT GROUP

A support group provides an opportunity for personal growth from a situation that might otherwise be simply stressful. In work with the dying and grieving it is essential to develop some form of peer support to alleviate stress, prevent burnout, and provide an outlet for emotional reactions. Often a group is an appropriate form.

Members must be committed to the group, and commitment levels should be relatively equal so that one person does not dominate. Group members need to be open to giving and receiving appropriate feedback. If someone is not willing to participate in a support group, Kara does not accept her as a counselor.

The counselor support groups at Kara have found that successful leadership can come from an experienced counselor with minimal additional training. The leader takes a low profile by serving as a group facilitator and coordinator. She also meets weekly with the other coordinators and the Director. The coordinators are the heart of Kara; they help plan training sessions, supervise casework, and focalize their groups. Every six months new coordinators are elected by the counselors, although they tend to be re-elected for a one-year term.

Kara counselors meet with their groups at least once a week, finding that this helps to prevent burnout and provides an opportunity for on-going training as well. But most of all it provides a place for the counselor continually to "meet himself" and learn about his relationship to this work. This is one of a number of functions a support group can serve. The main goal is to meet the specific needs of the participants.

Following are a few exercises to help you assess your own potential for experiencing burnout.

Exercise: Personal Exploration of Anger and Depression

Description:

1. Answer the questions on anger and depression following.
2. Talk to a friend about your responses and reactions.

Reasons for Using:

Anger and depression are two common emotions in the dying and grieving. It is important for the counselor to understand his own relationship with these emotions.

Materials:

Questionnaire.

QUESTIONS ON ANGER AND
DEPRESSION FOR COUNSELORS

1. How do I express my anger?
2. How do I repress my anger?
3. How could my relationship with anger interfere with others?
4. How has anger come up for me during these days of dealing with death and grief?
5. How do I respond when others express anger?
6. What do I need to learn about my ability to express or repress anger?
7. What happens to me physically when I feel depressed?
8. What do I want when I'm depressed?
9. What does my depression need from me?

Exercise: How Much Stress Are You Under?
(Holmes-Rhae Life Events Scale) from: Kay Carpenter, Palo Alto, CA, © 1982. Reprinted by permission.

Time: Unlimited

Description:

1. Look at the *Holmes-Rhae Life Events Scale* following.
2. For each listed event that you have experienced in the last 12 months, give yourself the corresponding number of points. If that event occurred twice, give twice the points.
3. Add up the points, then calculate your risk of getting sick, depressed, or having an accident according to the categories at the left: 0 - 199 points times the percentage.
4. What does this tell you about your life right now?
5. What changes do you want to make to take care of yourself?
6. If you were counseling a widow who was debating selling her house, how might you use what you have learned from this exercise?
7. How do you feel about your life right now? Does your total score help explain why? Are you surprised? Alarmed? Skeptical about your score?

Reasons for Using:

1. To determine the risk you run of burning out, getting sick,

depressed, or having an accident.

2. To determine how much loss there has been in your life the last year.
3. To determine how much more you need to take care of yourself.
4. To identify why you might be feeling the way you do, if you are tired or burned out.
5. To identify stress that you are not aware of.

Materials:

Copies of *Holmes-Rhae Life Events Scale* (following).

Notes:

1. Resist the temptation to see events as good or bad. Participants may say "Yes, but some of these are happy events, not all are bad or stressful." Any change implies a loss of some kind. Change, whether experienced positively or negatively, requires adaptation, therefore it becomes a stressor. Remember, stress is a *response,* not an event from outside the individual.
2. When in doubt, take the points each time the event is experienced. Remember, stress is cumulative.

THE SOCIAL READJUSTMENT RATING SCALE*

Life Event	Mean Value
1. Death of spouse	100
2. Divorce	73
3. Marital separation from mate	65
4. Detention in jail or other institution	63
5. Death of a close family member	63
6. Major personal injury or illness	53
7. Marriage	50
8. Being fired at work	47
9. Marital reconciliation with mate	45
10. Retirement from work	45
11. Major change in the health or behavior of a family member	44
12. Pregnancy	40
13. Sexual difficulties	39
14. Gaining a new family member (e.g., through birth, adoption, oldster moving in, etc.)	39

15. Major business adjustment (e.g., merger,
    reorganization, bankruptcy, etc.)   39
16. Major change in financial state (e.g., a lot worse off
    or a lot better off than usual)   38
17. Death of a close friend   37
18. Changing to a different line of work   36
19. Major change in the number of arguments with
    spouse (e.g., either a lot more or a lot less than
    usual regarding child-rearing, personal habits, etc.)   35
20. Taking out a mortgage or loan for a major purchase
    (e.g., for a home, business, etc.)   31
21. Foreclosure on a mortgage or loan   30
22. Major change in responsibilities at work (e.g.,
    promotion, demotion, lateral transfer)   29
23. Son or daughter leaving home (e.g., marriage,
    attending college, etc.)   29
24. Trouble with in-laws   29
25. Outstanding personal achievement   28
26. Wife beginning or ceasing work outside the home   26
27. Beginning or ceasing formal schooling   26
28. Major change in living conditions (e.g., building a
    new home, remodeling, deterioration of home
    or neighborhood)   25
29. Revision of personal habits (dress, manners,
    associations, etc.)   24
30. Trouble with boss   23
31. Major change in working hours or conditions   20
32. Change in residence   20
33. Changing to a new school   20
34. Major change in usual type and/or amount
    of recreation   19
35. Major change in church activities (e.g.,a lot more
    or a lot less than usual)   19
36. Major change in social activities (e.g., clubs, dancing,
    movies, visiting, etc.)   18
37. Taking out a mortgage or loan for a lesser purchase
    (e.g., for a car, TV, freezer, etc.)   17
38. Major change in sleeping habits (a lot more or
    a lot less sleep, or change in part of day
    when asleep)   16
39. Major change in number of family get-togethers
    (e.g., a lot more or a lot less than usual)   15

40. Major change in eating habits (a lot more or a lot less food intake, or very different meal hours or surroundings)   15
41. Vacation   13
42. Christmas   12
43. Minor violations of the law (e.g., traffic tickets, jaywalking, disturbing the peace, etc.)   11

---

*Source: Holmes, T.H. and Rahe, R.H.: The Social Readjustment Rating Scale, *Journal of Psychosomatic Research 11:*213-218, 1967. Reprinted by permission.

PREVENTIVE MEASURES

The following suggestions are for using the Social Readjustment Rating Scale for the maintenance of your health and prevention of illness:*

    1. Become familiar with the life events and the amount of change they require.

    2. Put the Scale where you and the family can see it easily several times a day.

    3. With practice you can recognize when a life event happens.

    4. Think about the meaning of the event for you and try to identify some of the feelings you experience.

    5. Think about the different ways you might best adjust to the event.

    6. Take your time in arriving at decisions.

    7. If possible, anticipate life changes and plan for them well in advance.

    8. Pace yourself. It can be done even if you are in a hurry.

    9. Look at the accomplishment of the task as a part of daily living and avoid looking at such an achievement as a "stopping point" or a "time for letting down."

    10. *Remember,* the more change you have, the more likely you are to get sick. Of those people with 300 or more Life Change Units for the past year, almost 80% get sick in the near future; with 150 to 299 Life Change Units, about 50% get sick in the near future; and with less than 150 Life Change Units, only about 30% get sick in the near future.

So, the higher your Life Change Score, the harder you should work to stay well.

Exercise: What Can I Do To Take Care Of Myself?

Time: Unlimited

Description:

1. Complete the Holmes-Rhae Life Events Scale above. ("How much stress are you under?").
2. Look at your Holmes-Rhae score and your "Reasons I feel burned out" or something about your life that's stressful.
3. Generate as many ideas as you can of things to do to take care of yourself.
4. Prioritize.
5. Set a time goal and identify a first step.
6. Write all this down on a big sheet of paper. Post on wall or just share what you like with a friend.

Reasons for Using:

Identify how you can avoid and/or cope with burnout in your life.

Materials:

Pen, large sheet of paper, and masking tape for posting.

Notes:

1. Resist the temptation to see events as good or bad. *Any* change implies a loss of some kind. Change, whether experienced positively or negatively, requires adaptation, therefore it becomes a stressor. Remember, stress is a response, not an event from outside the individual.
2. When in doubt, take the points each time event is experienced. Remember, stress is cumulative.

Exercise: The Victim Position
from: Fredrick Van Rheenen, M.D., modified from Actualizations

Workshop, 1982. Reprinted by permission.

Time: Unlimited

Description:

1. Sit quietly for 5 minutes, shut your eyes, and remember a time when you felt victimized. Feel the details of that experience and what was happening around you at that time.
2. Now ask yourself: "How did I get them to do this to me?" (5 minutes).
3. Look at the Imposed Upon cycle following.

Reasons for Using:

1. To explore the experience of feeling like a victim and how to work with it.
2. To understand that even though we may feel like victims, we do participate in the relationship. When we realize this, we often feel more energized and in control of our life choices.

Materials:

Copy of *The Imposed Upon Cycle* following.

Notes:

1. This teaches how to overcome feelings of being victimized, both for yourself and for the client.
2. Notice how your energy changed with steps 1 and 2. Usually it becomes dark, angry or sad at first; and then vibrant in step number 2.

THE IMPOSED UPON CYCLE*

I. *Pattern of Behavior:*

       Attempt to meet everyone's needs
       Attempt to take care of everyone
       Do a lot for others
       Generous
       Can't say no
       Tendency to feel overwhelmed
       May be accompanied by a sense of urgency

II. *May Lead to:*

       Exhaustion
       Resentment
       Feelings of being
          unappreciated

IV. *Guilt*

III. *Anger:*

       Assertiveness
       Less skillful anger—blowup, rage,
         irritability, sarcasm, criticism,
         guilt-laying
       Turned inward—depression
       Converted to physical symptoms
         e.g., hypertension, pain,
         binge-eating
       Sense of entitlement—alcohol,
         drugs, affairs, debt

This cycle can be broken primarily in position I by setting limits. It can also be broken in position III by a clear and direct expression of what the person is experiencing.

*Source: Fredrick Van Rheenen, Palo Alto, Calif. 1982.

PEAK PERFORMANCE AS A POSSIBLE LIFESTYLE

Peak performance involves taking an active role in creating exactly the life you want to live. Dr. Charles Garfield, who has counseled hundreds of dying clients during the course of his work at Shanti, an organization in San Francisco, California, similar to Kara, found that some clients consistently beat the statistical odds for survival. This led him to examine what these survivors did to promote survival, then to look at individuals who were especially successful in life. The latter group seemed to have vast energy resources but were not workaholics. Rather, they were people whose relationship with themselves allowed them to perform beyond the norm.[4]

The lifestyle of these high performers, according to Garfield, included the following:

1. They spend at least two-thirds of their lives doing what they want to do, as compared to not doing what they want to do, or doing what they do not want to do. The words that describe their lives are "intentionality" and "enjoyment" as compared to the words "determination" and "relief" (when the task is done)—which describes a person who is not doing what he wants to do. Wanting to do things and not doing them is as stressful as doing things that you do not want to do.

2. The high performers spend a good deal of time structuring and managing their lives to make sure that they get to do what they want. They do what is necessary efficiently or they delegate it. As a result, they spend much of their time doing what they want. They are masters at working on a team, collaborating, and delegating.

3. They do not lead fragmented lives. Their survival work is also their life's work. In time management, they account for time to relax and time to be with their family. They also leave time for things that may come up that they cannot anticipate. They are not constantly managing crises.

4. High performers seem also to have good communication skills, and do not waste time mis-communicating. High performers are able to move beyond their current beliefs into new modes of understanding. They are flexible and accept creative possibilities.[5]

Dr. Garfield offers two exercises that are useful in assisting a counselor to develop the life he wants.

FIGURE 4
PEAK PERFORMANCE EXERCISE*

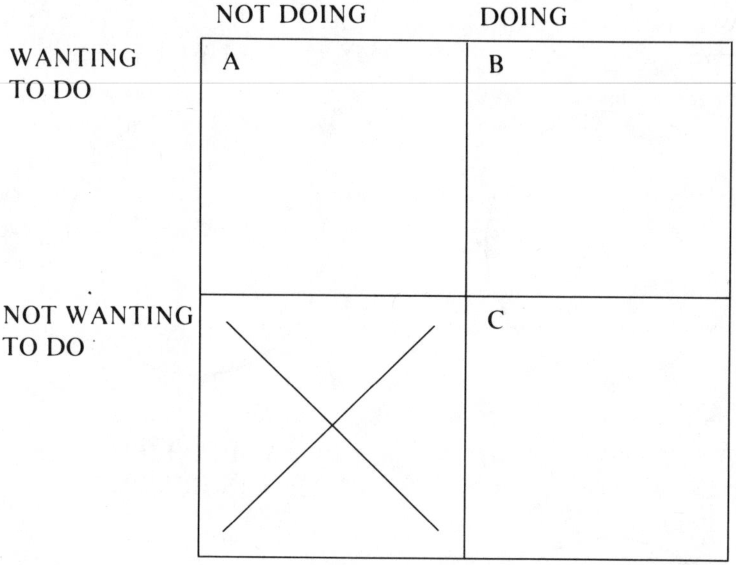

	NOT DOING	DOING
WANTING TO DO	A	B
NOT WANTING TO DO		C

Directions:

1. Read and fill out each quadrant as follows:

    A. What are you wanting to do in your life that you are not doing?
    B. What are you wanting to do and doing?
    C. What are you not wanting to do in your life that you are doing?

2. The counselor should fill each quadrant out twice: once for his work situation and once for his personal life.

Note: Peak performers are oriented to quadrant B.

*Source: Charles Garfield, Ph.D., Berkeley, Calif., 1982. Reprinted by permission.

FIGURE 5
PEAK PERFORMANCE EXERCISE*

HOW I SPEND MY TIME AT WORK:

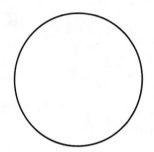

HOW I WOULD LIKE TO SPEND MY TIME AT WORK:

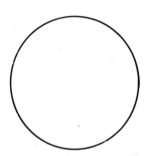

HOW I SPEND MY TIME IN GENERAL:

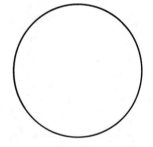

HOW I WOULD LIKE TO SPEND MY TIME IN GENERAL:

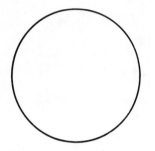

Directions:

Divide each circle into slices, with the size of the slice corresponding to each major time category. Are there big discrepancies? Anything new added? Is there a slice that is too big? Too small?

The high performer has a clear idea of how time is spent, and is a victim of "surprise attacks." All this is built into time management.

High performers know how to set limits and are not guilty when they say "no." They also know how to say "yes" with great enthusiasm. As a result, there is more opportunity to choose what they want to do in life.

*Source: Charles Garfield, Ph.D., Berkeley, Calif., 1982. Reprinted by permission.

REFERENCES

[1]Larson & Garfield, *Berkeley Hospice Training Manual,* Berkeley, Calif.: Berkeley Hospice Training Project, 1982.

[2]C. Garfield, "Impact of Death on the Health-Care Professional," in H. Feifel (ed.) *New Meanings of Death,* New York: McGraw-Hill, 1972.

[3]These causes and signs were compiled from several sources, including: W. Bryan, "Preventing Burnout in the Public Interest Community," *Grantsmanship Center News,* April 1981, pp. 15-75; C. Maslach, "Burned Out," *Human Behavior,* Sept. 1976, pp. 16-22, C. Maslach and A. Pines, "The Burnout Syndrome in the Daycare Setting," *Childcare Quarterly,* 6(2): 100-113, 1977; and D. Larson and C. Garfield, *Berkeley Hospice Training Manual,* Berkeley, Calif.: Berkeley Hospice Training Project, 1982.

[4]*Supra* note 2.

[5]*Supra* note 1.

CHAPTER EIGHT

PERSONAL EXPLORATION OF DEATH AND GRIEF

There have been a number of studies of the impact of death desensitization techniques involving personal exploration of death and grief. All but one report a reduction in anxiety about death and a change in attitude towards death as a result of increased personal death awareness. These changes in turn affect the participants' relationship with their work and their understanding of dying and grieving.

The following death awareness exercises consist of discussion, self-exploration, and role-playing to probe questions, feelings, confusions, concerns, beliefs, and experiences with death and grief. The counselor needs to know how death influences the lives of his clients, their families, and friends, as well as how it has influenced his own life and his understanding of mortality. Each counselor will have his own unique way of understanding death that derives from his personal history and character structure. The more he understands his own personal style, the less it will interfere unconsciously in interactions with clients.

In addition to learning and responding to the material in Chapters Two, Three, and Four, there are a variety of death exploration exercises that can help you to become aware of your own attitudes toward death. Some of the following exercises are similar, so you may want to choose those that best suit your needs and personal style. It is important to note that the exercises do not provide any new material, but instead are designed to draw out attitudes and feelings you already have and make you more aware of what is going on around you. After each exercise you should consider how what you have discovered about yourself may affect how you relate to people who are dying or grieving. This will aid movement towards personal authenticity and sensitivity in counseling.

A WORD OF CAUTION

Nearly every counselor, in the course of training for work with the dying and grieving, encounters the existential questions of meaning in life and becomes more aware of the fragility of existence. Occasionally, because of unresolved conflicts or life experiences, a trainee may undergo a major crisis of identity and purpose as a result of exploring his relationship with death. As resistances to awareness are overcome, intense anxiety may surface and previously unconscious fears may come to the fore.

Major life crises as result of training in death awareness are rare. But some of the exercises used at Kara do tend to bring up uncomfortable material, and the presence of a skilled trainer is advised. The exercises presented here have been selected as appropriate for individual or small group work, without a trainer present. A full complement of exercises is provided in a companion volume for trainers, *Dying and Grieving: A Trainer's Manual.*

Exercise: Lifeline

Adapted from: James Bugental, "Confronting the Existential Meaning of My Death Through Exercises," *Interpersonal Development*, 1973, *4*, pp. 148-163 © 1973 by James Bugental, Ph.D. Reprinted by permission.

Time: Unlimited

Description:

Take a piece of paper and draw a horizontal line. Mark two spots delineating your birth and your death. Now mark where you are currently. Take the space between your birth and now and mark five or six important choice points in your life that led you to where you are today. Now mark 5 or 6 choice points that you anticipate in your life in your future. Be somewhat realistic. We're talking about what you guess may actually occur in your life.

Describe to a friend why you picked the age you will die and what the turning points are in your life. What do you have still ahead of you in your life? Were there problems with putting the "now" x? Looking back at the choice points, do you notice any patterns in your choices? Do you see any choices that you can imagine now you would make differently?

In looking at the future: Was it hard to predict? Was it hard to separate what you wish would happen from your realistic predictions?

Reasons for Using:

An excellent way to focus on your current understanding of your life and mortality. A way to look at your purposes, priorities, and reasons for living.

Materials:

A large sheet of paper and crayons or markers.

Notes:

This exercise is useful in helping people to begin thinking about the fact of their own death and to evaluate their life goals.

Exercise: Personal Death Experiences

Time: Around 20 minutes

Description:

With a group of 3 to 5 friends, ask each other to consider what personal meanings you feel can be gained from exploring death and dying. If you have experienced the loss of someone close to you, what have you learned from that loss?

Reasons for Using:

Initiates discussion of personal losses, allows for personal sharing and catharsis.

Materials:

None.

Exercise: Time of Death

Time: Variable

Description:

1. Discuss with a friend: *"When* do you think you will die? What is the probability that you will die now, tomorrow, in 5 years, 10 years, 25 years, 50 years? *How* do you think you will die? *Where?* Will death sneak up on you, or will you know it's coming? Do you think you will be rebellious? Reconciled? Will you have a long-term illness or will it be sudden?"
2. Each of you should talk 15 minutes, 5 minutes sharing, then change places.

Reasons for Using:

To explore your attitudes toward and awareness of death.

Materials:

None.

Exercise: Angel of Death

Time: ½ hour

Description:

Respond to the following question by writing on a piece of paper or exchanging responses with a friend: "You have died. You have pleaded with the Angel of Death to be allowed to return to life. There are so many things you have yet to do. The Angel of Death grants you one additional week—no more. Imagine that tomorrow is the first morning of that extra week. What will you do? How will you spend that week?

Reasons for Using:

Helps you to look at "unfinished business" and at your current satisfaction with life. Uses death as the stimulator to be living as fully as you can now.

Materials:

None.

Exercise: Your Autobiography
Adapted from: P. Koestenbaum, *Is There an Answer to Death,* Englewood Cliffs, N.J., Prentice-Hall, 1976, pp. 82-83.

Time: 45-60 minutes

Description:

Write your autobiography, not just a statement of events, but:
1. For whom are you writing this autobiography?
2. How did you come to lead the life that in fact you did?
3. What can you teach others as a result of your life experiences?
4. What have you learned about yourself?
5. As a result of this, do you see your future goals any differently? What are they?
Discuss your autobiography with a friend or a group.

Reasons for Using:

Helps to increase awareness of life choices and satisfaction with them.

Materials:

Paper, pens.

Notes:

This is an interesting activity to do in a group. Spend 20 minutes writing, then talk about it.

Exercise: Writing Your Own Obituary
Adapted from: James Bugental, *Interpersonal Development,* 1973, 4, pp. 148-163. "Confronting the Existential Meaning of My Death Through Exercises." Reprinted by permission.

Time: 1 hour

Description:

1. Write your own obituary, reflecting who you actually are and the meaning of your life. What contributions have you made? What events stand out?
2. Discuss with a friend, who has also written his or her own obituary.

Reasons for Using:

Looking at how you define who you are.

Materials:

Paper, pens.

Notes:

Each person should read his obituary and candidly share what it means to him. You may be reluctant to portray your true real self, and need to be given feedback on how your friends perceive you.

The discussion should move into a more global explanation of your thoughts in general about death.

Exercise: Poetry or Essays

Time: Unlimited

Description:

Write a poem or essay expressing feelings about or experiences with death. Or if you prefer to work with visual materials a painting or collage. See example following.

Reasons for Using:

Personal expression of a response to death or grief.

Materials:

Paper, large and small, paints or crayons or pastels, tape.

Example:

Where Are You, Marge?*

The withered faces greet
Visitors with vacant eyes.
Yesterday's meatloaf and urine
Permeate the air. I will not
Eat another carrot.

Only my right side works, allowing
Me a continous cigarette. Each
Pleasurable draw crowding my growth-
Infested lungs. I want to go home.
Away from this place where families
Send pictures instead of visit.

It's only 8 a.m. and old Charlie makes his
Fifth trip past my door.
The screams of ancient Annie mingle
With "Good Morning, America".
Horses are lucky, they shoot them.

*Source: Diana Platt, Burlingame, Calif. 1982. Reprinted by permission.

Exercise: Exploration of Death

Time: Varied

Description:

1. Do this with a small group of friends or colleagues.
2. Hand out the following questionnaire and instruct everyone to look over the questions, write out responses, then discuss the issues together.

Reasons for Using:

These questions will stimulate new insights and understanding about your own feelings and an awareness of the variety of other people's viewpoints.

Materials:

Questionnaire.

Notes:

These are valuable questions to bring home to your family. One Kara counselor filled out these questions and died suddenly a few months later. Her family found her responses and used them in her memorial service. They were very touched to read her notes to them. For her, what had been "just an exercise" became a reality.

QUESTIONS ON DEATH AND GRIEF

1. What is your spiritual viewpoint about death and immortality? What factors in your life drew you to this belief?
2. Do you believe in life after death? In what form? Is there a part of you that will live forever?
3. Have you ever had or witnessed a near-death experience?
4. Talk about loss and letting go. Look at the patterns of how you've handled this in your life, not only with people, but with other loved objects.
5. What was your earliest loss? How did that affect you?
6. Have you known anyone who committed suicide? How do you react to suicide?

7. Have you known anyone who was murdered? What was your reaction?
8. The thing that frightens you the most about dying is _____ . (Look at the act of dying rather than death itself.)
9. What visual image do you have about your death?
10. How have your feelings about death changed in the past year, five years, ten years?
11. What would you be willing to give up in order to live? What parts of your body, what body functions?
12. How would you like to die? Is your fantasy realistic?
13. When did you first realize that you will die?
14. Do you want to be cremated or buried? Have you talked about this with family members?
15. Have you told friends and family what kind of funeral service or memorial service that you want? Give details.
16. Take a piece of paper and make a rough draft of what you would like to say to special people in your life. Tell them your special thoughts about them.

Exercise: Disidentification/Orpheus Experience

James Bugental, *Interpersonal Development*, 1973, 4, pp. 156-161 © 1973 by James Bugental, Ph.D. Reprinted by permission.

Time: 1 to 1½ hours

Description:

Have ready 10 pieces of paper (3x5 cards are fine) and a pencil. Find a comfortable relaxed place for yourself in the room. Have a friend read the following text to you after you both listen to quiet, peaceful music for ten minutes. Use a friend who is sensitive to you. This will be a powerful experience for both of you.

Friend read: "Please take ten pieces of paper and number them in the upper right-hand corner. There's a reason, as you'll see, for using a particular corner. When you've done that, take a minute or so to get comfortable and in touch with yourself, your own center. [Pause a minute or so then continue.] Now I am going to ask you *one* question to which I'd like to have you write ten answers. Remember *ten different answers to one question.* Your answers may be words, phrases, sentences, whatever satisfies you that you have given ten different answers to my question. Put one answer on each sheet of paper and work fairly rapidly without too much deliberation. One thing you should know is that no one but you will see your answers, so let your answers be quite spontaneous and personally meaningful to you. The question is, 'Who are you?' "

[When this task is completed, ask]: "Please be sure to have ten numbered sheets of paper, each having a different answer to my question, 'Who are you?' [Pause.] Now, I'd like you to imagine as vividly as possible the following: suppose some power could so intervene in your life that one of your answers would no longer be true of you in any way. Which answer would you yield up to be changed first or most readily? [Repeat the supposition and the question.] Write a number '1' in the upper left-hand corner of that answer."

[Pause.] . . .

"And now decide which answer you would protect from being changed until the very last, which one you'd protect most of all. Put a '10' in the upper left-hand corner of that one."

[Pause.] . . .

"And now arrange the other eight answers between the number '1' and the number '10' so that number '2' in the upper left-hand corner becomes that answer you'd be next most, second most, willing to have changed for all time, number three is third, and so on."

[Pause.] . . .

"Now please check that you have your ten answers piled up with the number '1' in the upper left-hand corner on top, then number '1' and so on to number '10' in the upper left-hand corner, which is the one you'd least readily change and is on the bottom of the pile."

[Pause.] . . .

"Nearly every ethical or religious tradition so far as I am aware, has some concept of the importance of transcending or relinquishing the self . . . We can easily see how this must tie into the interpretation of death as a letting go of much or all of that which has made up our lives. What these mystical traditions add is what others too have recognized: that this relinquishment may be the basis for a heightened vitality or meaningfulness in living. Now I invite you to explore this important realm for yourself . . .

"Here is what we will do: in a minute I will ring this bell, so— [ring bell]. When I do, get comfortable physically and try to get in touch with your center, with your own being. Don't look at the papers yet. You may lie down or sit, as you find best. I suggest you close your eyes. Then, after a bit, I will ring the bell again. [Ring it.] When I do, look at your first answer, the one with the number one in the upper left-hand corner. Try to get a kind of total, organismic awareness of what that answer has meant in your life. For instance, if I saw that my first answer was my name, 'Jim', I might . . . hear my name as though it were spoken and discover that I had some kind of feeling around my face. I might then find I had other associations to it also. The point is to discover whatever comes naturally, spontaneously as I am aware of what that name, 'Jim', has meant in my life. There is no value in having many or few associations. It is disruptive to feel the need to press for more associations.

"Having gotten in touch with these associations, I then want to relinquish this way of identifying myself. This means that, in a way as I might take off this sweater I'm wearing and set it aside, I will take off being 'Jim'. I will try to feel not being 'Jim' anymore, ever again. Please notice this point; it's important: I want to relinquish being 'Jim' without offering myself a substitute—for example, being 'Tom' or some other name—just the letting go of that identity, feeling that as fully as possible.

"After you've felt into letting go of your topmost answer to the 'Who are you?' question, just stay quietly in your own center until you hear the bell again [ring it]. Don't go on to the next answer until the bell rings. If the bell rings before you have finished with the first answer, then let go of it and move on to the second.

"At the sound of the bell, look at your second answer—the slip with the '2' in the upper left-hand corner. Now repeat the process of letting go, as you did with the first answer. Find your associations to that aspect of your identity, then take them off, let go of them. Don't substitute something else, just let go of that way of being you. When you're finished get centered again and wait for the next bell.

"In this way we'll go through all ten answers. Yes, I know that it will be very hard to let go of some of the last of these, but do what you can. I think you will find it a meaningful experience.

"When you have finished the period for your tenth answer, I will ring the bell once again. This is for a final period in which you are just to stay quietly in your center and let happen within you whatever needs to occur. For some people this is a time of grief, but it is important sadness to confront. For some, this is a period of liberation. There is no right thing for it to be for you. For some people it is simply a quiet time and perhaps a chance for reflection. Just see what it is for you. When this last period is over, I'll ring the bell again, and then I'll suggest what we can do next . . .

[Ring the bell for the first time period.]

"All right, let's start. Please use this first period to get settled and to find your own center. Don't look at any of your answers yet. I'm going to stop talking in a minute, and I won't speak again until we've run though the whole ten answers. I don't want my voice to intrude on you. In the same way, please don't you talk during the experiment.

[After 2 minutes or so . . . ring the bell . . . A period of 90 seconds for each of the answers is about right for most people . . .]

[Ring bell again after about two minutes, then allow about 90 seconds for each answer. After the period for the tenth answer allow at least 2 full minutes for the experience of having relinquished all identity.]

"Many people find in the process of relinquishing these parts of our identity that some we had thought were so essential are not that important or that others we had thought trivial turn out to be among the most difficult to let go . . . Look through your ten answers again, and pick out that one you are *most anxious* to put back on, to reclaim as part of who you are. When you have found it, put a '1' in the lower left-hand corner of that slip.

"Now find the answer that you are *least anxious* to put back on again, to accept as part of your identity. Remember you must put them all back on. When you have found this answer that you are *least anxious* to have again, put a '10' in the lower left-hand corner of its slip.

"Now arrange the other eight answers between these two and number them so that the new, lower left-hand corner sequence runs from those you really are very anxious to reclaim to those you are relatively less concerned to have. Then put your slips in that sequence with the number one slip on top and the number ten on the bottom."

[Pause]

"Now we are going to go through a sequence very similar to the one we used a few minutes ago. In a minute, I'll ring this bell again [ring it], and then you may get settled into your center again. Don't look at your slips at that time. Just settle into your center and get in touch with how you felt when you had let go of all those ten aspects of your identity. [Pause.] Then when I ring the bell again, look at the first slip, the one

189

with the number '1' in the lower left-hand corner. This time you are to imagine as fully as you can how it feels to *choose* that as your identity. The important word is, 'choose'.

"Let me just say a word about that so you can see why it is so important. In so many regards, the ways in which we think of our own being seem to be imposed on us rather than chosen by us. If I think of my name, my parents gave it to me; I did not select it. If I think of the fact that I am a man or even a human being, that seems a product of biology not something of my own doing. Feeling that way about ourselves contributes to our feeling that we are powerless about what matters most in who we are. Today, let's see if we can experience it differently. Try to experience your own choicefulness for each of these answers.

"And that is not just a myth. My name was given me by my parents, to be sure, but I could change it, and I certainly can decide by which of its forms—'Jim, Jimmie, James', and so on—I will choose to be known. The fact that I am a human being really doesn't restrict me greatly. I can choose how I will express being human. And so on. There are infinite possibilities of choice in all of the aspects of my being.

"So as you look at your first slip, settle back into yourself and find your choicefulness in reclaiming it as a part of your identity. Don't work out the details; just feel it as something you have taken on yourself.

[Pause.] . . .

"Now some of the latter slips may have parts of yourself you don't want back or that you want only in changed form. For the moment, take each one as you originally wrote it. Don't change it now. Recognize that the first step in being able to change something about yourself is the acceptance that it is part of you and that you are the one choosing to have it so. Later on we'll talk about how you might change it.

[Pause.] . . .

"You will hear the bell and settle down into your center. At the second bell you will look at the slip numbered '1' in the lower left-hand corner and find your choice to have it true of you. Then you will stay quietly in your center until you hear the next bell. When you hear it, you will look at the slip numbered '2' in the lower left-hand corner. Again you will take it on choicefully. And so on through the pack. When you've finished the slip numbered '10' in that lower left-hand corner, there will be one additional period. Use that just to stay quietly with yourself, discovering where you are and what your feelings are. Ready? Here's the first bell. [Ring it.] Get settled now and don't go to the slips until you hear the next bell.

[For this phase, use somewhat shorter intervals. With most people, one full minute seems right. At the last interval, which comes after the minute for answer number 10, allow 2 or 3 minutes. At the end of this last period, quietly invite your partner to share his experience. This discussion usually turns out to be a rich and varied one. It may take any of a number of directions: sharing introspective experiences, discussing the personal meanings that death has, recognizing the ways what we value begins to change when we are faced with giving it up, valuing the aliveness and immediacy of the moment, etc.]

If your partner asks about the remaining corner of the slips, respond with something like this:

"Yes, there's one more possible experience. Having had a little taste of the underworld or of what death may mean, we may decide we're not satisfied to continue just as we always have. This is an individual thing, and there's no reason anyone has to make such a decision. If you feel that way, you may want to use that last corner to rework the priorities of your life. What do you want to put first? What is relatively unimportant? What do you want to change? The space is blank. The choice is yours—you've already exercised your choicefulness in taking each of these parts of your identity back. It's up to you."

Exercise: Death Visualization
Adapted from: Kay Carpenter, Kara counselor

Time: 45 minutes or variable

Description:

Find a friend. Ask him or her to read this out loud slowly to you:

"First of all, make yourself comfortable and relax. Loosen any tight clothing. Close your eyes and repeat to yourself the word 'relax.' Breathe slowly.
"Relax. Deep breath - visualize the number '3', three times. [wait] Breathe - visualize the number '2', three times. [wait] Inhale - visualize the number '1', three times; exhale. [wait] Inhale 10, 9, 8 on exhale, inhale 7, 6, 5 on exhale. [wait] Inhale 4, 3, 2, 1 on exhale. [wait] Watch

191

your whole body relaxing - picture your head to toes in relaxation. [pause]

"Become aware that you are lying on a warm, sunny beach or floating in a warm pool on an airmattress ... direct all your attention in a very relaxed way to the feeling of sinking on the warm sand or floating, weightless, on the surface of water ... Feel the warm sun on your skin ... Feel the soft breeze ... smell the freshness of the air ... hear the lapping of water ... the sky is clear blue, the sun radiates ... feel the heat on your body ... hear the sound of your heart beating ... hear the sound of your own breathing ... breathe slowly and repeat the word 'relax'. Let it go ... let go of your feet, etc. ... (continue this progressive relaxation).

"When you are ready, allow yourself to imagine the following:

Three weeks ago you took a routine physical. Then one morning a couple of weeks later a nurse called. She said, 'We've found something in the blood tests and the doctor would like to do some more studies.' That was just seven days ago. You've spent all week taking more tests. Now, you're sitting in the doctor's office. Imagine what it is like as you wait: look at the walls, the furniture. Listen to the sounds. Become aware of your own breathing, of the feeling in your body. The doctor enters; says hello. There is a funny look on his face. He says that you have the most severe form of acute adult leukemia. You hear chemotherapy ... chances to live one year at most ... become aware of the voice tone ... You leave the office and return home.

"Imagine what is happening to you ... What are your thoughts and feelings? What are you feeling in your body?"

[Pause for three minutes]

"This perhaps is your final year of life. How do your family and friends respond to your illness? One by one, picture each of your loved ones and imagine his or her response. What do you tell them? How do they look? What do they say? How do you feel?"

[Pause 1 minute]

"Try to decide who will be your support system. Who will be the closest to you? Who will be most afraid and withdraw? Picture your spouse, parents, children, friends. What feelings do you have? You see them come closer or withdraw. What do they say or do? How do you feel?"

[Pause 5 minutes]

"Now you're a seriously ill cancer patient; what emotions do you feel as you try to live your remainder time? What do you do? How do you feel?"

[Pause 3 minutes]

"What thoughts and feelings do you have about dying as your time runs out?

"Now you lie awake at night unable to sleep. Imagine how it feels as you ask yourself: What has been the purpose of my life? What is the meaning of it now?

"As you feel what it's like to be dying, what words most accurately describe your life and what it means to you? What feelings are you most aware of?"

[Pause 2 minutes]

"When you are ready, become aware of the face of someone you love. It may be a child . . . a family member . . . a spouse . . . a lover . . . What feelings do you have about that person? What do you experience in your body? As you look at this person, become aware of what you have to say . . . life is slipping away. Your time is short. Go up to that person and establish contact in some way . . . tell that person what you have to say . . ."

[Pause]

"Now become aware that time has run out . . . it is time to say good-bye . . . feel yourself drawing gradually back . . . farther . . . feel yourself floating upward out into the sunlight . . . experience the sun's heat drawing you upward . . . feel the sun evaporating your body . . . feel your being rising upward into the soft blue sky . . . up toward the warm sun.

"From this point, look back on yourself, healthy and whole, lying here in this room. What you've just experienced is a dream, yet no less real than your daily life. When you are ready, return to your body here and now. Feel your aliveness, hear your blood running through your body; the sound of your breathing, your thoughts beginning again.

"When you are ready, become aware of your aliveness, here and now."

[Pause 1 minute]

"When you are ready, come back into the room ... gently open your eyes when it feels right."

Discuss this experience with each other.

Exercise: Boundaries

Time: Variable

Description:

1. Sit quietly for awhile and assess what you are feeling after completing this exploration of your personal relationship with death. Now ask several friends to join you.
2. Describe an imaginary line 10 feet long across the floor in front of you. The far left end represents feeling very close to people, willing to be intimate and social. The far right end represents feeling separated from people, wanting solitude.
3. Ask your friends to move along this line for a few minutes until they find a spot that represents how they feel in this movement. After they have settled, it is your turn to move along the line and find your spot. Try several positions, if you like.
4. Each of you ask yourselves how you feel in the position you selected. Are there judgments? What does it feel like to be next to someone when in this position? Does this position reflect a pattern in your life? How might this reflect your work with clients?

Reasons for Using:

To develop an ability to notice one's personal boundaries. To physically and visually understand your feelings about this work.

Note:

The position you choose is constantly changing in your life. There is no one good or right place to be. What is important is to notice your own response to being in that position.

AFTERWORD

This book has been about the experience of transition and how we respond to it. Death and birth are considered life's major transitions, but we need to remember we are in transition each moment we are alive. Many of these changes, like that of moving from the in-breath to the out-breath or of falling asleep and reawakening, occur so often that we no longer experience them as transitions. However, when we encounter a more difficult or unique transition we often expect ourselves to move through it with the ease of breathing or waking up, forgetting that we have never experienced it before.

What I wish for each of us in whatever transition we are moving through right now, and in our more difficult transitions, is that we will remember to be gentle with ourselves as we encounter the unknown. And I wish for us to also remember to love what is essential in ourselves and others as we watch each other move through changes. The poet Rainer Maria Rilke described it this way:

> "... I want to beg you, as much as I can, to be patient toward all that is unsolved in your heart and to try to love the *questions themselves* like locked rooms and like books that are written in a very foreign tongue. Do not now seek the answers, which cannot be given you because you would not be able to live them. And the point is, to live everything. *Live* the questions now. Perhaps you will gradually, without noticing it, live along some distant day into the answer.
>
> "Resolve to be always beginning—to be a beginner."[2]

REFERENCES

[1] M. Whelan and M. Warren, "A Death Awareness Workshop: Theory Application and Results," *Omega Journal,* 11(1): 61-71, 1980; T. Laube, "Death and Dying Workshops for Nurses: Its Effect on Their Death Anxiety Level," *International Journal of Nursing Students,* 14: 111-120, 1977; P. Murray, "Death Education and Its Effects on the Death Anxiety Level of Nurses," *Omega Journal,* 35: 1250, 1974.

[2] John J.L. Mood (trans.) *Rilke on Love and Other Difficulties: Translations and Considerations of Rainer Maria Rilke.* New York: W.W. Norton, 1975, p. 25.

BIBLIOGRAPHY

DEATH: GENERAL BOOKS

Adler, C.S., Stanford, G., & Morrissey, A.S. *We are but a moment's sunlight.* New York: Washington Square Press, 1976.

Becker, E. *Denial of death.* New York: Macmillan, 1973.

Cantor, R.C. *And a time to live.* New York: Harper & Row, 1978.

Choron, J. *Death and modern man.* New York: Collier Books, 1972.

Choron, J. *Death and western thought.* New York: Macmillan, 1963.

Feifel, H. (Ed.). *The meaning of death.* New York: McGraw-Hill, 1959.

Feifel, H. (Ed.). *New meanings of death.* New York: McGraw-Hill, 1977.

Garfield, C. *Psychosocial care of the dying patient.* New York: McGraw-Hill, 1978.

Grollman, E.A. *Concerning death: a practical guide for the living.* Boston: Beacon Press, 1974.

Kalish, R. *Death, grief and caring relationships.* Monterey, Ca.: Brooks/Cole, 1981.

Keleman, S. *Living your dying.* New York: Random House, 1974.

Kübler-Ross, E. *On death and dying.* New York: Macmillan, 1969.

Kübler-Ross, E. *Questions and answers on death and dying.* New York: Collier Books, 1974.

LeShan, L. *You can fight for your life.* New York: M. Evans, Co., 1977.

Rollin, B. *First you cry.* New York: Signet Books, 1976.

Schneidman, E.S. *Death: current perspectives.* New York: Mayfield, 1976.

Simonton, M. *Getting well again.* Los Angeles: J.P. Tarcher, 1978.

Sontag, S. *Illness as metaphor.* New York: Farrar, Straus & Giroux, 1978.

Stoddard, S. *The hospice movement.* New York: Vintage Books, 1978.

Toynbee, A. (Ed.). *Man's concern with death.* New York: McGraw-Hill, 1968.

Watts, A. *Death.* Millbrae, Ca.: Celestial Arts, 1975.

Weisman, A. *On dying and denying.* New York: Behavioral Publications, 1970.

GRIEF AND LOSS

Bowlby, John. *Attachment and loss* (Vol. 1, Attachment). New York: Basic Books, 1969.

Bowlby, John. *Attachment and loss* (Vol. 2, Separation, Anxiety and Anger). New York: Basic Books, 1973.

Bowlby, John. *Attachment and loss* (Vol. 3, Loss). New York: Basic Books, 1980.

Caine, Lynn. *Widow.* New York: Bantam Books, 1974.

Jackson, Edgar N. *Understanding grief: its roots, dynamics, and treatment.* Nashville: Abingdon Press, 1957.

Jackson, Edgar N. *You and your grief.* New York: Hawthorne Books, 1962.

Jackson, Edgar N. *Telling a child about death.* New York: Hawthorne Books, 1965.

Jackson, Edgar N. *When someone dies.* Philadelphia: Fortress Press, 1971.

Jackson, Edgar N. *Coping with the crisis in your life.* New York: Hawthorne Books, 1965.

Jackson, Edgar N. *The many faces of grief.* Nashville: Abingdon Press, 1977.

Kries, B., & Pattie, A. *Up from grief.* New York: Seabury Press, 1969.

LeShan, E. *Learning to say goodbye: when a parent dies.* New York: Macmillan, 1976.

Lewis, C.S. *A grief observed.* New York: Bantam Books, 1961.

Moro, Ruth. *Death, grief and widowhood.* Berkeley: Parallax Press, 1979.

Morris, S.M. *Grief and how to live with it.* New York: Grosset & Dunlap, 1972.

Parkes, C.M. *Bereavement: studies of grief in adult life.* New York: International Universities Press, 1972.

Pincus, L. *Death and the family: the importance of mourning.* New York: Vintage Books, 1974.

Schiff, H.S. *The bereaved parent.* New York: Crown, 1977.

Schoenberg, B., Carr, A.A., Kutscher, A.H., Peretz, D., & Goldberg, I.K. *Anticipatory Grief.* New York: Columbia University Press, 1975.

Tatelbaum, J. *The courage to grieve.* New York: Lippincott & Crowell, 1980.

Westberg, G.E. *Good grief.* Philadelphia: Fortress Press, 1977.

Wylie, B.J. *Beginnings: a book for widows.* Toronto: McClelland and Stewart Ltd., 1978.

Yates, M. *Coping: a survival manual for women alone.* Englewood Cliffs, NJ: Prentice-Hall, 1976.

CANCER

LeShan, L. *You can fight for your life*. New York: M. Evans Co., 1977.

Rollin, B. *First you cry*. New York: Signet Books, 1976.

Rosenthal, T. *How could I not be among you?*. New York: George Braziller, 1973.

Simonton, C., & Mathews, S. *Getting well again*. Los Angeles: J.P. Tarcher, 1978.

PSYCHOLOGY OF DEATH

Aries, P. *Western attitudes toward death from the middle ages to the present*. Baltimore: Johns Hopkins University Press, 1974.

Cantor, R.C. *And a time to live: toward emotional well-being during the crisis of cancer*. New York: Harper & Row, 1978.

Cousins, N. *Anatomy of an illness as perceived by the patient: reflections on healing and regeneration*. New York: W.W. Norton, 1979.

Garfield, C.A. (Ed.). *Stress and survival: the emotional realities of life-threatening illness*. St. Louis: The C.V. Mosby Company, 1979.

Glaser, B.G., & Strauss, A.L. *Awareness of dying*. Chicago: Aldine, 1965.

Glaser, B.G., & Strauss, A.L. *Time for dying*. Chicago: Aldine, 1968.

Grof, S., & Halifax, J. *The human encounter with death*. New York: E.P. Dutton, 1977.

Kalish, R.A., & Reynolds, D.K. *Death and ethnicity: a psychocultural study*. Los Angeles: University of Southern California, Ethel Percy Andrus Gerontology Center, 1976.

Kastenbaum, R., & Alsenberg, R. *The psychology of death*. New York: Springer Publications, 1972.

Kavanaugh, R.E. *Facing death*. Los Angeles: Nash Publishing, 1972.

LeVine, S. (Ed.). *Death row: an affirmation of life*. San Francisco: Glide Publications, 1972.

Lewis, C.S. *The problem of pain*. New York: Macmillan, 1962.

Lifton, R.J. *Boundaries: psychological man in revolution*. New York: Macmillan, 1962.

Oyle, I. *The new American medicine show: discovering the healing connection*. Santa Cruz, Ca.: Unity Press, 1979.

Pattison, E.M. *The experience of dying*. Englewood Cliffs, NJ: Prentice-Hall, 1977.

Schultz, R. *The psychology of death, dying, and bereavement*. Reading, Pa.: Addison-Wesley, 1978.

Worden, J.W. *Grief counseling and grief therapy.* New York: Springer Publications, 1982.

DEATH AND SPIRITUALITY

Budge, E.A.W. *The Egyptian book of the dead.* New York: Dover Publications, 1967.

Castaneda, C. *Journey to Ixtlan: the lessons of Don Juan.* New York: Simon & Schuster, 1972.

Dass, R., & LeVine, S. *Grist for the mill.* Santa Cruz, Ca.: Unity Press, 1976.

Evans-Wentz, W.Y. *The Tibetan book of the dead.* New York: Oxford University Press, 1960.

Frankl, V. *Man's search for meaning.* Boston: Beacon Press, 1963.

Gold, E.J. *American book of the dead.* Nevada City, Ca.: I.D.H.H.B., Inc., 1978.

Goldstein, J. *The experience of insight.* Santa Cruz, Ca.: Unity Press, 1976.

Grof, S., & Halifax, J. *The human encounter with death.* New York: E.P. Dutton, 1978.

Holck, F.H. (Ed.). *Death and eastern thought: understanding death in eastern religions and philosophies.* Nashville: Abingdon, 1974.

Huxley, A. *The doors of perception.* New York: Harper, 1963.

Huxley, L.A. *This timeless moment.* New York: Farrar, Straus, & Giroux, 1968.

Kapleau, P. (Ed.). *The wheel of death: a collection of writings from zen buddhist and other sources on death-rebirth-dying.* New York: Harper & Row, 1971.

Keleman, S. *Living your dying.* New York: Random House/Bookworks, 1978.

Kübler-Ross, E. *Death: the final stage of growth.* Englewood Cliffs, NJ: Prentice-Hall, 1975.

Lao, Tzu. *The way of life* (W. Bynner, trans.). New York: Capricorn Books, 1962.

Leary, T., Metzner, R., & Alpert, R. *The psychedelic experience (a manual based on the Tibetan book of the dead).* New York: University Books, 1964.

LeVine, S. *A gradual awakening.* Garden City, NY: Anchor Press/Doubleday, 1979.

Lewis, C.S. *The great divorce.* New York: Macmillan, 1946.

Lewis, C.S. *A grief observed.* London: Farber & Farber, 1961.

Moody, R. *Life after life.* Atlanta: Mockingbird Books, 1975.

Moody, R. *Reflections on life after life.* Atlanta: Mockingbird Books, 1977.

Moss, T. *The probability of the impossible: scientific discoveries and explorations in the psychic world.* Los Angeles: J.P. Tarcher, 1974.

Osis, K., & Haraldsson, E. *At the hour of death.* New York: Avon Books, 1977.

Paardi, M.M. *Death: an anthropological perspective.* Washington, D.C.: University Press of America, 1977.

Pike, J.A., with Kennedy, D. *The other side: an account of my experience with psychic phenomena.* Garden City, NY: Doubleday, 1968.

Ring, K. *Life at death: a scientific investigation of the near-death experience.* New York: Coward, McCann & Goeghegan, 1980.

Suzuki, S. *Zen mind, beginner's mind.* New York: Weatherhill, 1970.

Tillich, P. *The courage to be.* New Haven: Yale University Press, 1952.

Toynbee, A. et al. *Man's concern with death.* New York: McGraw-Hill, 1968.

White, S.E. *The unobstructed universe.* New York: Dutton, 1940.

DYING—PERSONAL ACCOUNTS

Alsop, S. *Stay of execution: a sort of memoir.* Philadelphia: J.B. Lippincott, 1973.

Bermann, E. *Scapegoat: the impact of death-fear on an American family.* Ann Arbor: University of Michigan Press, 1973.

de Beauvoir, S. *A very easy death.* New York: Warner Books, 1964.

Evans, J. *Living with a man who is dying: a personal memoir.* New York: Taplinger Publishing, 1971.

Gunther, J. *Death be not proud: a memoir.* New York: Harper & Row, 1965.

Hanlan, A. *Autobiography of dying.* Garden City, NY: Doubleday, 1979.

Hine, V. *Last letter to the pebble people.* Santa Cruz, Ca.: Unity Press, 1979.

Ipswitch, E. *Scott was here.* New York: Delacorte Press, 1979.

Lee, L. *Walking through the fire: a hospital journal.* New York: E.P. Dutton, 1977.

Lerner, G. *A death of one's own.* New York: Simon & Schuster, 1978.

Pauley, D. Slow death: one survivor's experience. *Omega Journal,* 1977, 8(2), 173-179.

Rodman, F.R. *Not dying.* New York: Random House, 1977.

Rollin, B. *First you cry.* New York: Signet, 1976.

Rosenfeld, S.S. *The time of their dying.* New York: W.W. Norton, 1977.

Rosenthal, T. *How could I not be among you?.* New York: George Braziller, 1973.

Turnage, M., & Turnage, A. *More than you dare to ask: the first year of living with cancer.* Atlanta: John Knox Press, 1976.

Weingarten, V. *Intimations of mortality.* New York: Alfred A. Knopf, 1977.

Wertenbaker, L.T. *Death of a man.* Boston: Beacon Press, 1974.

West, J. *The woman said yes: encounters with life and death.* New York: Harcourt Brace Jovanovich, 1976.

DEATH IN LITERATURE

Agee, J. *A death in the family.* New York: Bantam Books, 1969.

Castaneda, C. *A journey to Ixtlan: the lessons of Don Juan.* New York: Simon & Schuster, 1972.

de Beauvoir, S. *A very easy death.* New York: Warner Books, 1964.

Gristofer, M. *The shadow box (a play).* New York: Avon Books, 1977.

Guest, J. *Ordinary People.* New York: Ballantine, 1980.

Huxley, A. *Island.* New York: Harper & Row, 1962.

Jury, M., & Jury, D. *Gramp.* New York: Grossman Publishers, 1976.

Olsen, T. *Tell me a riddle (short stories).* New York: J.B. Lippincott, 1961.

Panger, D. *The dance of the wild mouse.* Entwhistle Books, 1979.

Sarton, M. *A reckoning.* New York: W.W. Norton, 1978.

Schneidman, E.S. *Voices of death.* New York: Harper & Row, 1980.

Tolstoy, L. *The death of Ivan Illych and other stories.* New York: Oxford, 1960.

Zindel, P. *The pigman* (a novel). New York: Dell Publications, 1968.

CHILD'S UNDERSTANDING OF DEATH
AND WAYS OF SUPPORTING CHILDREN

Bluebond-Langner, M. "I know, do you?": A study of awareness, communication and coping in terminally ill children. In Carr, Goldberg, Kutscher, Peretz & Schoenberg. *Anticipatory grief.* New York: Columbia University Press, 1974.

Desey-Spinetta, P.M., Hartman, G.A., Loenig, H.M., Kung, F.H., Lightsey, A.L., Schwartz, D.B., & Spinetta, J.J. *Talking with children with a life-threatening illness: a handbook for health care professionals.* San Diego: Childhood Adaption Project, 8001 Frost Street, San Diego, CA 92123.

Grollman, E.A. (Ed.). *Explaining death to children.* Boston: Beacon Press, 1967.

Jackson, E. *Telling a child about death.* New York: Channel Publishing Co., 1965.

Sternberg, F., & Sternberg, B. *If I die and when I do: exploring death with young people.* Englewood Cliffs, NJ: Prentice-Hall, 1980.

Wilcox, S., & Sutter, M. *Understanding death and dying: an interdisciplinary approach.* Palo Alto, Ca.: Mayfield Publishing Co., 1981.

Yalom, I. *Existential psychotherapy.* New York: Basic Books, 1980.

TALKING WITH CHILDREN ABOUT DEATH

Bernstein, J.E. *Loss and how to cope with it.* Boston: Houghton Mifflin Co., 1977.

Center for Attitudinal Healing. *There's a rainbow behind every dark cloud.* Tiburon, Ca.: Center for Attitudinal Healing, 1978.

Grollman, E.A. *Talking about death: a dialogue between parent and child.* New York: Harper & Row, 1970.

Langone, J. *Death is a noun: a view of the end of life.* Boston: Little, Brown & Co., 1972.

Pringle, L. *Death is natural.* New York: Four Winds Press, 1977.

Stein, D.B. *About dying: an open family book for parents and children together.* New York: Walker & Co., 1977.

DEATH OF A CHILD

Becker, R.A. "Portrait of Jen: Memories from the children's cancer ward." In S.G. Wilcox & M. Sutton (Eds.), *Understanding death and dying.* Sherman Oaks, Ca.: Alfred Publishing Co., Inc., 1981.

Bleubond-Langer, M. *The private worlds of dying children.* Princeton, N.J.: Princeton University Press, 1978.

Easson, W.M. *The dying child: management of the child or adolescent who is dying.* Springfield, Il.: Charles C. Thomas, 1981.

Gunther, J. *Death be not proud: a memoir.* New York: Harper & Row, 1979.

Gyulay, J. *The dying child.* New York: McGraw-Hill, 1978.

Lund, D. *Eric.* Philadelphia: J.B. Lippincott, Co., 1974.

Miles, M.S. *The grief of parents.* Oak Brook, Il.: Compassionate Friends, 1978.

Schiff, H. *The bereaved parent.* New York: Crown Publishers, Inc., 1977.

Schweibert, P., & Kirk, P. *When hello means goodbye: a guide for parents whose child dies at birth or shortly after.* University of Oregon Health Sciences Center, 3181 SW San Jackson Park Road, Portland, OR 97101.

Sharkey, F. *A parting gift.* New York: St. Martins Press, 1982.

Stevenson, N.C., & Straffon, C.H. *When your child dies: finding the meaning in mourning.* Cleveland: Philomel Press, 1981.

Sturge, J. *The spirit of Scott.* c/o Sturge, 18 Lodge Pole Road, Pittsford, NY 14534, 1978.

Van Eys, J. *Humanity and personhood.* Springfield, Il.: Charles C. Thomas, 1981.

BURNOUT

Artiss, K.L., & Levine, A.S. "Doctor-patient relation in severe illness." *New England Journal of Medicine,* 1973, *288,* 1210-1214.

Dempsey, D. *The way we die.* New York: Macmillan, 1975.

Edelwich, J., & Brodsky, A. *Burnout: stages of disillusionment in the helping professions.* Human Science Press, 1980.

Freudenberger, H.J. "Staff burn-out." *Journal of Social Issues,* 1974, *30,* 159-165.

Freudenberger, H.J. *The staff burn-out syndrome.* Washington, D.C.: The Drug Abuse Council, 1975.

Freudenberger, H., & Richelson, G. *Burnout: the high cost of high achievement.* Garden City, NY: Anchor Press/ Doubleday, 1980.

Hay, D., & Oken, D. "Psychological stresses of ICU nursing." *Psychosomatic Medicine,* 1972, *34,* 109-118.

Lief, H.I., & Fox, R.C. "Training for detached concern in medical students." In H.I. Lief, V.F. Lief & N.R. Lief (Eds.), *The psychological basis of medical practice.* New York: Harper & Row, 1963.

Maslach, C. *"Detached concern" in health and social service professions.* Paper presented at annual convention of the American Psychological Association, Montreal, August 1973.

Maslach, C. Burned-out. *Human Behavior,* September 1976, *5,* 16-22.

Maslach, C., & Pines, A. "The burn-out syndrome in the day care setting." *Child Care Quarterly,* Summer 1977, in press.

Mechanic, D. *Public expectations and health care.* New York: John Wiley, 1972.

Pattison, E.M. "Psychosocial and religious aspects of medical ethics." In R.H. Williams (Ed.), *To live and to die: When, why and how.* New York: Springer-Verlag, 1974.

Pines, A., & Aronson, E. *Burnout: From tedium to personal growth.* New York: The Free Press, 1980.

Pines, A., & Maslach, C. *"Detached concern" in mental health institutions.* Paper presented at Annual Convention on Child Abuse, Houston, April 1977.

Pines, M. Psychological hardiness, the role of challenge in health. *Psychology Today,* December, 1980.

Potter, B. *Beating Job Burnout.* San Francisco: Harbor Publishing, Inc., 1980.

Selye, H. "They all looked sick to me." *Human Nature,* February, 1978.

Sheppe, W.M. Jr., & Stevenson, I. "Techniques of interviewing." In H.I. Lief, V.F. Lief & N.R. Lief (Eds.), *The psychological basis of medical practice.* New York: Harper & Row, 1963.